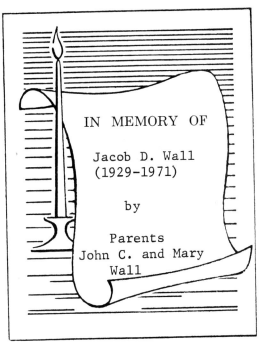

IN MEMORY OF

Jacob D. Wall
(1929-1971)

by

Parents
John C. and Mary
Wall

D1733367

*Monograph Supplements to the*
*Scottish Journal of Theology*

General Editors

T. F. TORRANCE and J. K. S. REID

◁━━━▷

# INDIA AND THE LATIN CAPTIVITY
# OF THE CHURCH

# IN THIS SERIES

BR
1155
B66

# INDIA AND
# THE LATIN CAPTIVITY
# OF THE CHURCH

## THE CULTURAL CONTEXT OF
## THE GOSPEL

### R.H.S.BOYD

*Vice-Principal, Gujarat United School of Theology*
*Ahmedabad, India*

CAMBRIDGE UNIVERSITY PRESS

13014

HIEBERT LIBRARY
PACIFIC WITHDRAWN SEMINARY

Published by the Syndics of the Cambridge University Press
Bentley House, 200 Euston Road, London NW1 2DB
American Branch: 32 East 57th Street, New York, N.Y.10022

© Cambridge University Press 1974

Library of Congress Catalogue Card Number: 73-86049

ISBN: 0 521 20371 6

First published 1974

Printed in Great Britain
by R. & R. Clark Ltd, Edinburgh

FOR HONOR AND BILL

# CONTENTS

# PREFACE

This book is based on a series of lectures given in the Presbyterian College, Belfast, in February and March 1972. I am grateful to the Very Reverend J. L. M. Haire, Principal of the College, to the other members of the Faculty, and to the students of the College for their kindness and hospitality. I also wish to thank the Reverend Professor T. F. Torrance of New College, Edinburgh, and the Reverend C. K. Young, Convener of the Foreign Mission of the Presbyterian Church in Ireland, for much help and encouragement.

ROBIN H. S. BOYD

Ahmedabad
November 1973

# NOTE ON TRANSLITERATION
## OF INDIAN WORDS

(1) Indian language words have been transliterated with standard diacritical marks. As a rough guide to pronunciation the following points should be noted:

> a is a short, almost indistinguishable sound, like the a in *patrol*.
> ā is a full a, as in *past*
> c is pronounced ch, as in *chit*
> ś is pronounced sh, as in *she*
> ṣ is also sh, though the sound is produced differently
> s is like English s, as in *say*

(2) Proper names have been given in their familiar English form, even though this may not be strictly correct as a transliteration, e.g. Krishna, Keshub Chunder Sen.

(3) In quotations, the transliterations are those of the original author.

# INTRODUCTION

The background of this book is eighteen years of life in India, most recently as a teacher of theology and a presbyter of the Church of North India. Also in the background is Belfast, the city where I was born and grew up. This background explains the frequency of references to Northern Ireland, and to a particular part of India – the State of Gujarat.

For many people in India and elsewhere the inter-communal violence in Northern Ireland is symbolic of the failure of western Christianity – its failure to live by the Gospel, and to share that Gospel with others. And today voices from India are being heard in the West, voices which claim that there are other ways than the way of Christ. But Indian Christian voices are also being heard. Has Christian India a significant message for the western Church – a message which might help to restore fellowship between antagonistic groups, to deepen the Church's understanding of the Gospel, and to make its communication of that Gospel more effective?

The tradition which the English-speaking Churches of the West have inherited is inevitably Graeco-Roman, and more especially Latin, and it is difficult for an Anglo-Saxon or Celtic Christian to look at his faith and practice except through Latin spectacles. The Indian Church has been strongly influenced by this same tradition, inherited from western missionaries, yet today it is emerging with its own distinct and fascinating cultural identity. Has this Indian Church anything to say to the West which will enable the West to rediscover its faith in a wider and richer context? Can the western Church break out of its bondage to Greek philosophy, to the Latin language, and to Roman structures?

The title of one of Luther's best known anti-Roman polemics

speaks of the Babylonish captivity of the Church. More than four centuries later the western Church – reformed and Roman Catholic alike – is still constricted by its dependence on a single cultural tradition. Has India a message of freedom for the Latin captivity of the western Church?

# 1

INDIA AND THE GOSPEL –
PATTERNS OF RESPONSE

Since the day of Pentecost the Christian Gospel has had a profound and sustained confrontation with three great cultural
traditions.[1] The Church's beginnings were in the Jewish world,
where Christ came to his own people to fulfil their expectations
as Messiah, or, in the penetrating phrase of the Reformers, as
prophet, priest and king. The Jewish Church was soon absorbed in something much larger, but it has left its permanent
and essential mark on the universal Church, in the Scriptures,
in theology, in forms of worship and in the structures of the
Church.

Then came the confrontation with Graeco-Roman culture, a
process which began even before Pentecost, when certain
Greeks came to Philip saying, 'Sir, we would see Jesus,' and
when officers of the Roman army of occupation brought their
problems to the young Jewish religious leader. The book of
Acts and the letter to the Galatians tell the story of what happened after some eager Jewish Christians from Cyprus and
North Africa decided one day to preach to a group of Greeks
in the city of Antioch.[2] The Gospel was for all men, and the
writers of the New Testament realised that Greek would be a
more effective medium for their testimony than Aramaic. It
was not long before the Church was thoroughly at home in the
Graeco-Roman world, carrying out its missionary and apologetic task in the language and thought-forms of that world.
It was a world of which we ourselves are the heirs – with a

[1] Cf. R. C. Zaehner, *At Sundry Times* (1958), pp. 165ff.
[2] Acts 11. 19–21.

I

judicious but diluted admixture of Celtic, Teutonic and Saxon additives.

Since that first confrontation there have of course been many others, for example with the world of Islam, with China, and today with the quasi-religion of Marxism. Islam, however, like Communism, has deep roots in the Judaeo-Christian tradition. In China, one of the ingredients of the cultural situation was Buddhism, itself an offshoot of Hinduism; in any case, it is hard to say whether the cultural interpenetration of Christianity in China will ever be resumed in its old form, since China seems today to have by-passed its own traditions. And so we come to the third great and continuing confrontation of the Gospel, that with Hinduism. Here we have a culture which, though it contains a strong Indo-European element, is vastly different from Europe; a self-contained and self-sufficient culture with a quite astonishing wealth of forms in religion, philosophy and art. The interaction of Christianity with Indian culture has been extensive enough and prolonged enough for something new and interesting to emerge, and it is the implications of that encounter which we hope to study in this book.

The Christian faith began in the Middle East. Many Indians, however, regard it as a western religion, the religion of the materialistic peoples of Europe and America. And for that reason they reject it. It seems to come as a threat to their own culture, and to the many fine and stabilising traditions which that culture enshrines. 'What right have western missionaries to come to India and try to spread a faith which has got itself enmeshed in a culture so inferior to our own?' they say. And today there are many in the West who would accept this diagnosis; many who would go further and say that the Christian faith, and above all the institutional Christian Church, have nothing to say to mankind; who would hold perhaps that there are voices today – and silences – from India itself which offer greater promise to the West than does the preaching in a thousand pulpits.

But what about *Christian* India? Have Indian Christian voices anything to say to us in the West? I believe they have.

### The Christian approach to the Hindu

First of all let us glance very briefly at the attitudes of the different groups of Christian missionaries who have worked in India down the years.

Christianity reached India very early. Tradition says that the Apostle Thomas himself went to India and died there. Certainly there has been a Christian Church in Kerala in South India since the third century, and probably considerably earlier. It was a Syrian Church, owing allegiance to Antioch, with a liturgy in the Syriac language, and with a theology classified by theologians as monophysite or Eutychean.[3] Later the Nestorian Church of Persia also established work in India as part of that astonishing missionary outreach which began about the end of the fourth century. So we find that the theological divisions of the early Church – for example that between Eutycheans and Nestorians – take a denominational form in India right at the beginning of the story.

We know little of the missionary methods of these early Christians. The tradition is that as a result of the preaching of Thomas and others a number of high caste families became Christian. A strong Christian community was eventually established in Kerala, but until comparatively recently it was rather introspective, living more or less as a separate caste within the Hindu milieu, and with little or no concern for evangelism; the main question was one of survival. Relations with Hindus were mainly good, but depended on rigid separation – not unlike, for example, the position of the Jews in European society. Gradually the caste-structure of the surrounding Hinduism came to affect the Church; the Church on the whole, however, had little effect on Hindu society.

The first missionaries of the western Church to reach India were some friars – four Franciscans and a Dominican who arrived in 1321, all but the Dominican meeting their death by martyrdom at Thana near what is now Bombay. The main

---

[3] Monophysitism – the doctrine that in Jesus the divine and human elements combine to form a single nature (*mone phusis*).

thrust of the Roman Catholic mission, however, began at the beginning of the sixteenth century, and was closely linked with the outreach of Portuguese imperialism. In 1514 Pope Leo X established the *Padroado*, an arrangement which gave the Portuguese crown rights over 'the Christians of the East', and the Christianising of India was accepted as one of the aims of the imperial policy. So began an association between Christianity and imperialism which was destined to have a very counter-productive effect on the work of the Christian mission. The establishment of the Inquisition in India did not help matters. Francis Xavier, the great Jesuit missionary who came to India in 1542 and stayed for ten years, was an energetic and dedicated evangelist, yet there is no doubt that the general policy of the Portuguese mission was to use the power of the sword to promote the expansion of the Church. This power was used not only upon Hindus, but also on the Syrian Christians, many thousands of whom were persuaded in various ways to come over to the Roman obedience, usually with the sacrifice of their Syriac liturgy, and the adoption of the Latin rite.

Not all the Jesuit missionaries, however, were happy with this policy, and Roberto De Nobili, who arrived in 1605, was a notable exception. Realising that Hindus regarded Christianity as a foreign import he adopted the dress and style of a Brāhmin *sannyāsi*, set himself to learn Sanskrit – the first European to do so – and used his knowledge of the Hindu scriptures to communicate the Christian faith in language and thought-forms which would be intelligible to those whom he hoped to reach. His mission in Madurai was successful, but his ecclesiastical superiors were afraid of the possible effects on the traditional structures of the Church, and the experiment was short-lived, though it has never been forgotten.

The first Protestant missionaries to India were the German Lutherans Ziegenbalg and Plütschau of the Danish Mission, who arrived in Tranquebar in what is now Madras State in 1706. It is a very strange thing that nearly two hundred years had to elapse after the beginning of the Reformation in 1517 before the Protestant Churches awoke to their responsibility to carry the Gospel to non-Christian lands. In the English-speaking countries the awakening came even later, after the Methodist movement and the beginnings of the evangelical revival in England. The first British missionary to India was the redoubtable Baptist cobbler William Carey, who arrived in India in 1793, and, prohibited by the British East India Company from working in its territory, began his work on Danish soil at Serampore near Calcutta. Carey was not, of course, the first British Christian minister to set foot in India. The East India Company had had its own chaplains since the middle of the seventeenth century, but they limited their work to the pastoral needs of their white compatriots. Protestant Christians, in the shape of Dutch and British merchants, had been there for the people of India to see ever since the establishment of the first British 'factory' at Surat in 1608, but the people of India had not been at all impressed by these meat-eating, wine-drinking, violent characters whose way of life seemed to contradict all that they themselves understood by religion.

The Protestant missionaries in their approach to India rightly gave first priority to the translating of the Bible into Indian languages. Along with the work of translation and distribution went preaching. The main emphasis went, of course, on the positive proclamation of the Gospel; but in addition they made a careful study of Hinduism, which they proceeded to refute with that rational logic so beloved of the late eighteenth century. Public debates were held between missionaries and Hindus; controversial pamphlets were published; John Wilson of Bombay wrote a book called *The Exposure of Hinduism*. Along with this controversial approach went much very enlightened work for social reform in such matters as education, infanticide, *sati*,[4] and the improvement of the lot of women, and in this task the missionaries were soon joined by some outstanding Hindu leaders. The British authorities (until 1857 the East India Company) gave no official encouragement to the mission-

[4] The custom of the self-immolation of a widow on the funeral-pyre of her husband, sometimes spelt *suttee* in English. For the literal meaning of the word, see below, p. 87.

aries, and indeed until the revision of the Company's charter in 1813 they were positively discouraging, yet as the century wore on the prestige of the British *raj* undoubtedly gave a reflected glory to the work of the missionaries.

The theology of the early missionaries was the theology of their British supporters – evangelical Christianity with a firm admixture of critical, hard-headed rationalism which delighted in ridiculing the apparent illogicalities of other religions while remaining perhaps a little blind to the vulnerability of some of their own positions. This theological outlook continued on through the nineteenth century, and in some places continues more or less intact today. The later decades of the century did, however, bring a change of theological climate – just as they did in Europe – through the development of the critical study of the Bible, through the influence of the controversy over evolution, and through the growth of the study of comparative religion, a field in which the leading part, so far as India was concerned, was played by Max Müller. The result of this development was a much more sympathetic attitude towards Hinduism, seen at its best in J. N. Farquhar's book *The Crown of Hinduism* (1913), which is really an exposition of Jesus' words in Matt. 5. 7, 'I came not to destroy but to fulfil'.[5] In this book Farquhar analyses various types of Hindu spirituality, and then seeks to prove that in Christ all that is best in the Hindu tradition reaches its perfection. In Farquhar's words, 'Hinduism must die into Christianity, in order that the best her philosophers, saints and ascetics have longed and prayed for may live.'[6]

The Barthian outlook on non-Christian religions did not fully reach India until the publication of Hendrik Kraemer's *The Christian Message in a Non-Christian World* in 1938, but with that event a negative approach to Hinduism took over, and held the field for about twenty years. Since the late 1950s, and partly as a delayed result of the work of a group of Indian

[5] For a good account of Farquhar see Eric J. Sharpe, *Not to Destroy but to Fulfil* (Uppsala, 1965).
[6] Quoted in Sharpe, *ibid.*, p. 360.

theologians like Chenchiah who opposed Kraemer's view (whom we shall discuss presently) a new approach has gradually become prevalent, which for the sake of convenience we may describe as 'dialogue'.[7] Dialogue demands the abandonment of the attitude of hostility and its replacement by friendship and concern; it requires an informed knowledge of the beliefs and practices of the other faith, and the open 'sharing' of religious experience in an attempt to plumb the depths of each other's spirituality; only in such a context ought the Christian to witness to Christ and the place that Christ holds in his own life. This point of view – which of course has its opponents – has become familiar not only among Protestants but also – and with the blessing of Vatican II – among Roman Catholics.

### The Hindu response to the Gospel

We must now look at the other side of the medal and consider how Hindus have reacted to the work of Christian missions. Naturally enough the Portuguese imperialist approach created great hostility, though large numbers of people, especially in Goa, became Christian for various reasons. The response to Carey and the Serampore missionaries, who were not backed by military might, was rather different.[8] The Christian Gospel found an immediate response in Ram Mohan Roy (1772–1833), who was to become the first great Indian social reformer; he joined forces with the missionaries in attacking social abuses like *sati* and child-marriage, and at the same time made a detailed study of the Bible, being greatly drawn to the ethical teaching of Jesus, which he presented to his compatriots in 1820 in a book entitled *The Precepts of Jesus*. What Ram Mohan Roy wanted, however, was a highly ethical theistic faith and a great, but not divine, religious leader. This

---

[7] See Herbert Jai Singh (ed.), *Inter-Religious Dialogue* (Bangalore, 1967).
[8] See M. M. Thomas, *The Acknowledged Christ of the Indian Renaissance* (1969), for a good account of Ram Mohan Roy's controversy with the Serampore missionaries.

gave him an immediate point of contact with the Unitarians of England and America, and as a result we find that many of his writings sound extremely like what was emanating from the non-subscribing party in the contemporary Arian controversy in the West. Ram Mohan Roy never became a Christian, but instead founded his own brand of Hindu Unitarian Church, the Brāhma Samāj.

A later leader of the Brāhma Samāj, Keshub Chunder Sen (1838–1884), came much closer to an understanding of the Gospel; even more than Ram Mohan Roy he was gripped by the charisma of Christ. Unlike the somewhat cold and rationalistic Ram Mohan he had a warm and emotional temperament, and responded to the love and self-sacrifice of Christ, rejoicing that Christ was Asian and not the kind of European figure whom the missionaries seemed to portray. Unlike the Unitarians, also, Sen was greatly attracted to the doctrine of the Trinity, of which, as we shall see, he gave his own very original and Indian interpretation.

Both these great Bengalis reacted in a positive way to the Christian faith, yet at the same time there were many evidences of a more hostile reaction. It is well known that one of the causes of the Mutiny of 1857 was the fear that the government of the East India Company was going to encourage the forced conversion of Hindus to Christianity. And a doughty champion of the anti-Christian movement appeared in Swami Dayananda Sarasvati (1824–1883), who in 1875 founded the militantly anti-Christian Arya Samāj, a reformed Hindu sect which has had a far greater success than the Brāhma Samāj, and continues in full vigour today. It holds that the Aryan faith, revealed in the Vedas, is the proper faith for the Aryan people, and that foreign religions should be rejected.

Keshub Chunder Sen's approach to religions was syncretistic, and this view was given classic expression in the work of two more great Bengalis, one a humble saint, Sri Ramakrishna (1836–1886) and the other a consummate propagandist, his follower, Swami Vivekananda (1863–1902). They preached a harmony of all religions; the goal of all religions is union with

God, and all religions are equally viable roads for reaching it. In Ramakrishna's words,

I have practised all religions – Hinduism, Islam, Christianity – and I have also followed the paths of the different Hindu sects . . . I have found that it is the same God towards whom all are directing their steps, though along different paths.[9]

This view has become almost universal among educated Hindus, and has been given virtually official sanction through its association with Mahatma Gandhi. It also provides the rationale for the doctrine of the secular state, which is enshrined in the Indian Constitution. Gandhi, though remaining a Hindu, laid great stress on the need for respect for all religions, with the distinct implication, however, that no one should change his religion, but should seek instead to be the best that he could be within the bounds of his traditional allegiance.

Some Hindu thinkers have taken the argument a stage further, with the view that mankind is evolving towards a single universal religion, a 'world faith' which will be able to unite mankind. An interesting Gujarati thinker, Manilal C. Parekh (1881–1967), argued that this universal faith should be of the warm, theistic, devotional kind – what he calls the Bhāgavata Dharma – while Dr S. Radhakrishnan, the distinguished philosopher and former President of India, envisages a more intellectual, monistic faith which would approximate rather closely to Dr Radhakrishnan's own idealist reinterpretation of the *advaita* of Shankara.

It is clear, therefore, that the religious leaders of India have never felt inclined to a wholesale acceptance of the Christian Gospel. Their attitude has varied between outright rejection and polite tolerance; they see Christianity as one among a number of great theistic faiths, some of whose features might well form part of a coming world faith, but a religion which certainly does not live up to the exclusive claims made for it by its adherents. In the rather chilling words of Radhakrishnan, 'You Christians are very ordinary people making very extraordinary claims.'

---

[9] Quoted in *Cultural History of India* (Belur Math, Calcutta), II, 518.

## The rise of the Indian Church

Yet despite this rather discouraging response on the part of the leaders of Hindu thought, the Christian Church took root in India. In many areas the earliest converts were men of high caste who endured much persecution and ridicule, and were driven out by their own community.[10] Not a few of them had, like Sundar Singh, profound personal experiences, sometimes accompanied by visions and dreams; two of the early converts of the London Missionary Society in Gujarat, Girdhar and Kuber, were confirmed in their resolution to find out about the Christian faith by the appearance of a comet in the sky, and many similar stories of unusual religious experiences have been told.[11] It is estimated that less than a fifth of the Christians in India today are descended from these early high caste converts.[12] What of the other four-fifths? The accusation has been made that they were underprivileged people who were virtually bribed by the missionaries to become Christians, with the offer of education, medical help, employment and so on. This is a very sweeping charge. No doubt many people did become Christian with an incomplete understanding of Christian belief. There were times of famine, like that of 1900, when the missions saved thousands of children from starvation, and many, though not all, of them later became Christian. Yet the fact of the matter is that for thousands of outcaste and tribal people the entry into the Christian Church meant the opportunity to enter a sphere of warmth and humanity which Hinduism had for millennia denied them. The missionaries came with a vision of the meaning of the new humanity which Christ brings, and through their love and service they sought to put it into practice.

[10] Cf. Rajaiah D. Paul, *Chosen Vessels* (Madras, 1961), and, for Gujarat, R. H. Boyd, *The Tiger Tamed* (1936) and *Trophies for the King* (Belfast, 1953).
[11] William Clarkson, *Missionary Encouragements in Western India* (2nd edn, Surat, 1957).
[12] R. B. Manikam, quoted in Nirmal Minz, *Mahatma Gandhi and Hindu–Christian Dialogue* (Bangalore, 1970), pp. 85, 86.

And people responded to that practical demonstration. In the
words of M. M. Thomas, the missionaries

> became the bearers of social and cultural humanisation as their
> very approach to the outcastes with the gospel changed the spiritual
> foundations of the inbuilt structures of the caste system. Salvation
> in Christ became the source of a new human fellowship. . . . The
> outcastes, the poor and the orphans saw the Christian faith as the
> source of a new humanising influence and the foundation of a
> human community.[13]

The Indian Church has no cause to be ashamed of the Gospel
which made men of many whose humanity had been denied.

For these early Christians the break with the past was complete, and was symbolised by baptism which, while it marked
their entry into the Christian Church, was also regarded by their
former Hindu community as automatic self-excommunica-
tion. Some of the more sophisticated tended to adopt European
ways of life; others, like Nehemiah Goreh, did not. Although
this famous Brāhmin convert wrote a book entitled *The Rational
Refutation of Hinduism* (1862) his own style of life and way of
thought remained thoroughly Indian, and there were many like
him; while village Christians, and they were the great majority,
have maintained to this day a thoroughly Indian way of life.

There were problems for the new Christians, one of the most
difficult being that of caste. De Nobili in his Madurai mission
had accepted the principle of caste, and limited his own work
to the Brāhmins, so that eventually there were separate congregations for Christians of different caste-groups. The same
principle was followed, sometimes deliberately, sometimes as it
were by accident, in some of the Protestant Churches in South
India. In the North the problem of caste in the Church has
been faced more uncompromisingly. In the early days of the
Church in Gujarat, for instance, there was a famous occasion
at Borsad in 1844 when the missionary announced that all the
Christians would sit down together at the Lord's table and
drink from the same cup. Some could not take this breaking

[13] M. M. Thomas, *Salvation and Humanisation* (Bangalore, 1971), pp. 12,
14.

of caste, but those who did became the nucleus of the Church, and no division on grounds of caste has ever been allowed to break Christian fellowship.

Another difficulty can be summed up in the expression 'mission compound'. Those who became Christian were frequently driven out of their homes and lands and jobs, and tended to congregate around the missionary's bungalow, where gradually a little, isolated Christian community arose which had very little in common with its surrounding environment. This led to a sense of dependence on the mission, a tendency to regard the missionary as the Christian's 'Mā-bāp' (father and mother), and has led to an unhealthy separation between the Christian and the world around him, and at times to the charge that Christians were 'de-nationalised'.

The Churches which gradually came into being were naturally organised along the denominational lines of the missionaries themselves. In Gujarat, for example, a presbytery of the Presbyterian Church in Ireland was set up, and continued in existence till 1900.[14] To begin with, its ministerial members were all missionaries, although later Indian ministers were added, as guests. The organisation was uncompromisingly western, and so were the buildings which gradually began to dot the Indian landscape – first Georgian, and then from about 1850 changing to Gothic. The atmosphere was never entirely western, however, especially in the villages, and from early days Indian music was used, and the worshippers took off their shoes and sat on the ground, men on the right and women on the left.[15] On the whole, relations between the different denominations were good, but there were cases of sheep-stealing[16] and at times almost open warfare, as in a regrettable episode between the Salvation Army and the Irish Presbyterian missionaries in the 1880s. The general tendency, however, was

[14] R. H. Boyd, *The Prevailing Word* (Belfast, 1953), p. 143.

[15] In many areas there were missionaries with a keen interest in Indian architecture and design, e.g. J. Sinclair Stevenson of Gujarat, who used local wood- and stone-carving techniques with excellent effect.

[16] K. Baago, 'Sheepstealing in the 19th Century', in *Bulletin of the Church History Association of India*, 10 (1966), 17ff.

towards increasingly close co-operation, and a series of decennial missionary conferences beginning in 1872 led eventually to the adoption of the principle of 'comity', whereby the different Churches and societies divided out the country between them, to promote more effective work and to eliminate competition. The Edinburgh Missionary Conference of 1910 was a landmark on the road towards Christian unity and led in 1914 to the formation of the National Missionary Council, which in 1923 became the National Christian Council of India. Meantime, many Christians had become convinced that mere comity was not enough, and that the time had come to put into action Christ's prayer for his followers, 'that they all may be one' (John 17.21). Negotiations for a united Church in South India began in 1919, and in 1947 the Church of South India (CSI) was inaugurated. Things moved more slowly, but more comprehensively in the North; negotiations were begun in 1929, and the Church of North India (CNI), which includes Baptists as well as Anglicans, Methodists, Presbyterians, Congregationalists and others, was inaugurated at Nagpur on 29 November 1970.

## The Indian Church today

Christians in India today number about 14 million, roughly $2\frac{1}{2}$ per cent of the population, and of these about 5 million are Protestants, the remainder belonging to the various branches of the Syrian Church in Kerala and to the Roman Catholic Church. Christians are therefore the third largest religious community in the country, after Hindus and Muslims. Since 1947 India has been an independent republic, and its constitution guarantees to all citizens the right not only to practise but also to propagate their faith. The government has, however, imposed restrictions on the entry of missionaries into India, holding that the Indian Church should be self-supporting, and that it should no longer be necessary for it to be dependent on personnel from overseas. The percentage of Christians is highest among some of the hill tribes of Assam, such as the

Nāgās and Mizos, where whole communities have become Christian, and have reached a high level of self-support as well as of educational qualification. In the southern state of Kerala also, the home of the ancient Syrian Church, Christians account for about a third of the population. Over the rest of India, especially in the north and west, Christians are a very small minority, often less then one per cent of the total. Apart from a few leading families they tend to be mostly lower middle-class or working-class folk in the cities and small farmers or landless labourers in the villages. Not many Christians seem to have become wealthy in business or property.

Today the larger Churches, such as the CNI, are entirely self-governing, and the role of the foreign missionary is a minor one. Of the seventeen diocesan bishops of the CNI, for example, none are missionaries. The Church has not yet, however, succeeded in becoming financially self-supporting, even for such a vital thing as the salaries of its ministers, and many of the important and prestige-bringing institutions – colleges, hospitals, high schools and hostels etc. – require foreign money for their maintenance. This is obviously a weakness, and the Church is doing its best, through emphasis on stewardship, to right the balance, but in fact it is doubtful if a Church in an under-developed country can ever – or should ever – support so many institutions. It is not only the financial burden but also the burden in administration and personnel which at times proves crippling, and can divert the Church from its task of Christian witness. The Church is striving valiantly to carry on a tradition which goes back to the age of the western missionary, and many voices today are questioning the wisdom of this policy.

Although the number of missionaries at work in the so-called 'main-line' Churches has dropped drastically, the Churches continue at national level to maintain close contact with foreign mission boards. And in the many smaller missions and Churches of a more conservative evangelical complexion the dependence on foreign personnel and finance is even greater. Whereas the main-line Churches have handed over power and responsibility into Indian hands, some of these other groups have maintained the number of their foreign personnel and the high level of their control over finance and equipment, sometimes thus introducing a divisive element into the older Christian communities. This brings us face to face with one of the notable western-inherited divisions among Christians in India today – a division which troubles us in the West also – that between so-called ecumenicals and evangelicals. We shall be returning to this issue later; at the moment we simply mention it.[17]

Mrs Renuka Mukerji Somasekhar has written recently of the tension experienced by an Indian Christian 'whose Indianness is from his heritage of Indian culture and whose Christianity has come to him from a Graeco-Hebraic strain'.[18] This tension, with its quest for a new identity or 'selfhood' (to use the currently fashionable word) has had one very damaging result in the tendency towards faction and power-struggle which so often weakens the life of the Indian Church, and which no doubt has roots in other factors also, such as the survival in the Christian community of divisions connected with caste.[19] In a community with few outlets for its energy in political or civic life, it is natural if unfortunate that there should be in-fighting and power-struggles, even within the framework of a united Church; and not infrequently the very western structures of the Church, with their printed constitutions and graded series of Church courts, tend to provide situations which make quarrelling and litigation easy.

## Indigenisation

For many years there has been much talk about indigenisation of the Church, yet what has been accomplished so far has largely been experimental, and limited to a few areas, like theological seminaries or Christian conference centres. Protestant congregations, especially the more westernised city ones,

[17] See below, pp. 124ff.
[18] Renuka Mukerji Somasekhar, *Mission with Integrity in India* (New York, 1969), p. 16.
[19] For a realistic account of the Indian Church, see J. W. Grant, *God's People in India* (Madras, 1960); also Swami Abhishiktananda, *The Church in India* (Madras, 1969).

do not find it easy to accept innovations, and the Christian community is on the whole conservative – conservative in this case signifying reluctance to give up the western ways of worship which have been inherited from earlier, missionary-dominated generations. There have, however, been many interesting experiments in Indian types of worship, especially in some of the Christian *āshrams* or fellowship communities like that at Tirupattur in South India, where the beautiful chapel is built in the style of a Hindu temple, and the thoroughly Christian worship is designed to be of a form which will attract rather than repel a Hindu visitor. In many country areas it is traditional to have all-night open air meetings for the singing of Christian lyrics, often accompanied by dancing. At the recent inauguration of the CNI there was a cultural programme which included both classical and tribal dancing to illustrate various stories, and not a few western visitors felt that this programme brought them more into touch with the Indian tradition than did the very western order of service in the actual inauguration. Such dancing, especially among tribal people, has always been regarded as a normal expression of joy, and one not inconsistent with the approved norms of Christian life. Dr Edwin Orr, for example, has told of how in 1905 at a crowded presbytery meeting among the Khāsi people, 'singing overwhelmed the preaching, and many of the awakened people danced for joy, their arms outstretched, their faces radiant'.[20]

For many years the Roman Catholic Church, partly through its retention of Latin, lagged behind the Protestant Churches in the process of indigenisation. Since Vatican II, however, it has taken a great leap forward, and its more authoritarian structure has enabled it to do by a fiat from above what the more democratic Protestant processes might find difficult to persuade their congregations to accept. Most important has been the provision for a vernacular liturgy, including the use of the Scriptures in the vernacular; but in addition the use of certain Hindu customs and gestures has been encouraged, and the translations or adaptations of the liturgy have gone far ahead of the

[20] J. Edwin Orr, *Evangelical Awakenings in India* (New Delhi, 1970), p. 67.

Protestant Churches in the use of terminology and ideas borrowed – with Christian content read into them – from Hindu sources.

This ongoing process of indigenisation affects everyone – Roman Catholic and Protestant, ecumenical and evangelical – in varying degrees. It is important, for it shows that the Indian Church is conscious of the need to be thoroughly 'at home' in the Indian cultural context, and to get away from its inherited westernism. The Church in India today, caught as it is in this tension between its own inherited culture and the imported western tradition, is seeking to find its own identity, and the process of the search is sometimes a painful one. Voices from India, both Indian and foreign, have been raised in penetrating criticism of the westernness of the Church. Right at the beginning of the twentieth century the great Bengali theologian Brahmabandhab Upādhyaya wrote, 'Our Hindu brethren cannot see the subtlety and sanctity of our divine religion because of its hard coating of Europeanism. . . . They cannot understand how poverty can be compatible with boots, trousers and hats, with spoon and fork, meat and wine.'[21] Manilal Parekh was even more scathing in his book *Christian Proselytism in India: a Great and Growing Menace*, published in 1947. And more recently there have been those who, like the Danish theologian Kaj Baago, have felt impelled to withdraw altogether from the institutional Indian Church, convinced, like Charles Davis, that it was hindering the work of the Gospel.

That is a brief picture of how the Church has been planted in India, and where it stands today – at the end of the period of western dominance, and at the beginning of a new chapter. The outlines of that new chapter are still far from clear, but it is certainly going to be different from the old, as the Indian Church, discarding the unnecessary items of its western baggage, sets out on the next stage of its pilgrimage.

[21] Quoted in B. Animananda, *The Blade* (Calcutta, *c.* 1947), p. 74.

# 2

# THE DEVELOPMENT OF
# INDIAN CHRISTIAN THEOLOGY

## Shaping a terminology

We have seen something of how the Gospel came to India, what the reaction of the Hindu population was, and how the Christian Church gradually took root in Indian soil. We mentioned the work of Roberto De Nobili in Madurai in the early seventeenth century, and how he lived the life of a Brāhmin *sannyāsi*, learnt Sanskrit and Tamil, and wrote a number of interesting theological works. It would be wrong to imagine, however, that he really worked out an original Indian theology. Despite his success in coining new words and phrases in Sanskrit and Tamil to replace the Latin terminology on which he had been brought up, the theology which he produced was still that of the Council of Trent.[1] Later many Protestant missionaries were likewise to produce their expositions of the particular type of theology which they had brought to India. But first they had to tackle the problem of translating the Bible into the different languages of India. This presented many difficulties, not because of any lack of theological terminology, but because of its confusing and embarrassing richness. What word should be used for God, for example? The classical scholars opted for *deva*, which is cognate with the Greek *theos*

[1] J. L. Miranda, *The Introduction of Christianity into the Heart of India or Father Roberto De Nobili's Mission* (Trichinopoly, 1923), p. 22. Also Vincent Cronin, *A Pearl to India: the Life of Robert De Nobili* (1959). For a fuller account of the different theologians mentioned in this chapter see R. H. S. Boyd, *An Introduction to Indian Christian Theology* (Madras, 1969).

18

and Latin *deus*. But *deva* is often used in the plural for the different gods of the Hindu pantheon; was it suitable? Another word, used only in the singular, is *Iśvara*, which means the personal God, creator of the world. An excellent word, one would think, until a Hindu of the *advaita* (monist) tradition of Shankara points out that for him *Iśvara* is only a second-level form of God; God at his highest and truest is the unqualified Absolute, known as *Brahman*. What did the translators do? William Carey opted for *Iśvara*; but later revisions of the Bible, like the Gujarati one currently in use, changed this to *deva*; and now the latest translations – both Protestant and Roman Catholic – have gone back to *Iśvara* – rightly, I believe. On the whole the early translators tried to choose neutral words, and to avoid those with an obvious Hindu reference, and in this way a biblical vocabulary has been arrived at which Christians understand. Hindus, however, often find the Bible difficult, and are repelled by the strangeness of the terminology.

### Christian poetry

Some of the first Indian Christians to give literary expression to their beliefs were poets – and in this too they were following the path shown by De Nobili, and even before him by an interesting English Jesuit called Thomas Stephens, who had settled near the present Bombay in 1579 and written a Christian *Purāṇa* or folk-poem narrating Bible stories. One of the earliest Protestant poets was a Tamil called Vedanayaga Shastriar (*c.* 1790–1855), whose first poems – meditations on the birth and death of Christ – were published as early as 1813. Many poets followed in all the different language areas, the best known probably being Narayan Vaman Tilak (1862–1919) of Maharashtra. Here are two verses from one of his hymns:

> As the moon and its beams are one,
>   So, that I be one with Thee,
> This is my prayer to Thee, my Lord,
>   This is my beggar's plea.

> Take Thou this body, O my Christ,
> Dwell as its soul within.
> To be an instant separate
> I count a deadly sin.

There is a great deal of very Indian mysticism or *bhakti* in those lines.[2] Through the work of poets like these, Indian Christians gradually became familiar with the idea of expressing their Christian faith in the words and imagery of their Hindu background.

### *Keshub Chunder Sen* (1838–1884)

We have already noticed the name of Keshub Chunder Sen, the ebullient leader of the Brāhma Samāj who came so strongly under the spell of Christ although he never joined the Christian Church. Sen was a great lover of India, and felt that Christ's way to the heart of his fellow-countrymen did not lie through a Europeanised form of the Gospel. He once wrote:

Behold, Christ cometh to us as an Asiatic . . . and he demands your heart's affection. . . . He comes to fulfil and perfect that religion of communion for which India has been panting. . . . For Christ is a true Yogi, and he will surely help us to realise our national ideal of a Yogi.[3]

Sen was convinced that it was possible to expound the meaning of the Gospel in terms drawn from Indian religion. As we see from this quotation, he was anxious to commend Christ to his friends, and to show them that he came as the fulfilment rather than the rejection of their highest aspirations. We shall look briefly at two of his most constructive theological suggestions.

First, creation and the Logos. Here is what the Chandogya Upaniṣad (6. 2), written probably before 600 B.C., says about cosmic origins:

---

[2] J. C. Winslow, *Narayan Vaman Tilak: the Christian Poet of Maharashtra* (1930), p. 101.

[3] K. C. Sen, *Lectures in India* (1904), I, 388, 389.

In the beginning this world was Being, one only, without a second. It bethought itself: 'Would that I were many! Let me procreate myself!'

And here is Sen's account:

Here the Supreme Brahma of the Veda and the Vedanta dwells hid in himself. Here sleeps mighty Jehovah, with might yet unmanifested. . . . But anon the scene changes. Lo! a voice is heard. . . . Yes, it was the Word that created the universe. They call it Logos. . . . What was the creation but the wisdom of God going out of its secret chambers and taking a visible shape, His potential energy asserting itself in unending activities?[4]

Later we shall see that some of the early Fathers, notably the Apologists and Tertullian, said something very like that. Yet here the context is purely Indian, and the philosophical link-up goes back even earlier in the history of thought than the doctrine of the Logos used by the Fourth Gospel and the Fathers.

Secondly, let us look at what Sen says about the Trinity, a doctrine which, unlike Ram Mohan Roy, he accepted with enthusiasm. As we have seen, the highest Indian word which can be used for God, as the unqualified Absolute, is *Brahman*, which is not a proper name but a neuter noun. Traditionally, *Brahman* can be described only negatively – *neti, neti*, 'not this, not this'. And yet Indian thinkers have always held that there is one legitimate description of *Brahman*, as Being, Intelligence and Bliss (*Sat, Cit, Ānanda*). Here, said Sen – if we may use for the moment modern phraseology – is the 'model' we need in order to explain the very puzzling doctrine of the Trinity to Hindus. Just as *Brahman* has the inner relations of *Sat, Cit, Ānanda*, so God is revealed as the I AM (Being or *Sat*), as the Logos (*Cit*), and as the joy (*Ānanda*) and love of the Holy Spirit. No Hindu ever questions the unity of *Brahman*, so here we find a way of understanding the simultaneous unity and threeness of God which the biblical evidence requires Christians to believe. This is a most interesting exposition, which has been

[4] *Ibid.* II, 11.

further developed by later Indian theologians, especially Upadhyaya. It may seem strange to us, but is it any stranger than the Greek and Latin terms like *hupostasis* and *ousia, persona* and *substantia* with which we try to explain *our* understanding of the God we experience as triune?

## *Nehemiah Goreh* (1825–1895)

Not many Indian Christians accepted Sen's teaching at the time, and this is hardly surprising, as he remained outside the Church. And in fact in these very years an Indian champion of orthodox western Christianity arose in the person of Nehemiah Goreh, a Maharashtrian Brāhmin who after prolonged study and heart-searching, and after enduring much persecution, was baptised in 1848. A very sensitive and scholarly saint, Goreh devoted his life to unwearying advocacy of Christ and his Church, and to the 'rational refutation' (to quote the name of his best known book) of Hinduism and of Sen's reformed Brāhma Samāj. Goreh's apologetic, with its detailed inside knowledge of Hinduism, was effective, and it was through him that one of the most famous of Indian women, the social reformer Pandita Ramabai, came to Christ. His works remind one of Tertullian's *Adversus Praxean* or Origen's *Contra Celsum*. Yet he does not wholly repudiate his Indian heritage, and sees the Christian faith as the fulfilment of the best aspects of the old faith. In his meticulous Victorian English he writes,

May we, the sons of India, say, that the unity with God, Whom our fathers delighted to call 'Sat, Chit, Ananda Brahman', after which they ardently aspired, but in a wrong sense . . . yet after which they ardently aspired, God has granted us their children to realise in the right sense? Was that aspiration and longing, though misunderstood by them, a presentiment of the future gift? I indeed have often delighted to think so.[5]

Much of Goreh's energy was spent in controversy with the Brāhma Samāj. He felt that they were trying to advocate the

[5] N. Goreh, *On Objections against the Catholic Doctrine of Eternal Punishment* (1868), pp. 41–2.

ethics of Christianity while substituting a vague theism for the full Christian orthodoxy which he himself had come to accept. (After an early association with the Church Missionary Society he later became an Anglo-Catholic, and took a special delight in the Athanasian Creed – surely one of the few Indians ever to have done so!)

He did not reach his orthodox position on the Trinity without much mental struggle, and the story of how he finally got there is interesting. He found it hard to believe that Christ could be both a separate 'Person' and also divine. And strangely enough it was by beginning from the Holy Spirit that he was finally able to come to the belief that Christ is a separate Person of the Trinity. He based his argument on 1 Cor. 2. 11 (AV): 'What man knoweth the things of a man, save the spirit of man which is in him? Even so the things of God knoweth no man, but the Spirit of God.' He writes, 'As our spirits are not something separate from ourselves, so the Spirit of God . . . is not something separate from God.'[6] Other passages, like John 14, 16 etc., indicated to him clearly that the Spirit is in fact a distinct Person, and in this way he came to the idea of the Spirit as substantially one with the Father, yet a distinct Person. And having demonstrated this for the Spirit he was able to do the same for the Son. The similarity to Augustine's psychological analogy of the 'trinity' of the human consciousness – intellect, will and affection – will be noted. But Goreh would take nothing for granted, and had to convince himself of the truth of the doctrine of the Trinity. Afterwards, he was able to convince Pandita Ramabai of the same truth, at a time when she was being strongly tempted to become a unitarian.

### The three mārgas

According to Hindu spirituality there are three different *mārgas* or roads which lead to *mokṣa* or liberation – the state of union with God. The first and highest is the way of knowledge or *jñāna*, which leads to the overcoming of the mists of *māyā* and allows

[6] N. Goreh, *Proofs of the Divinity of our Lord* (1887), p. 2.

the human soul or *ātman* to realise its unity with the Supreme Soul, *Paramātman* or *Brahman*. The great exponent of this *mārga* was the eighth-century philosopher Shankara. There are, however, two other 'ways', that of devotion (*bhakti*) and that of action (*karma*). The way of *bhakti* is that of loving, even emotional devotion to a personal God who is revealed in an incarnation or *avatāra*. The devotee commits himself to God in total surrender, but the *mokṣa* which he experiences is that of loving personal union rather than of that absorption or identity which is found in Shankara (as indeed in some of the medieval Christian mystics like Eckhart). The great philosophical exponent of this way was Ramanuja, who lived in the late eleventh and early twelfth centuries. Just as, in the West, Christian theologians have allied themselves with different trends of philosophical thought Augustine with Plato, Aquinas with Aristotle, Barth (at least in his early period) with a type of existentialism, for example – so a number of Indian Christian theologians have found that the thought-forms of the three *mārgas* have provided them with different media for the expression of Christian belief. We shall take a brief look at the work of some of them.

### Brahmabandhab Upadhyaya (1861–1907) – *jñāna mārga*

We have seen how Nehemiah Goreh rejected Keshub Chunder Sen's teaching, partly no doubt because he knew that Sen was not totally committed to Christ, and also because some of Sen's ideas would not stand up to detailed logical analysis. But what would happen if there were a totally committed Christian, with a razor-sharp mind, who yet felt that Sen's approach was a sound one, but needed to be carried through with more theological skill and less mere emotion? Such a man was Upadhyaya, whose name we have already noted, and who was perhaps even more famous as a nationalist leader than as a theologian. He was born a Brāhmin, but later fell under the spell of Sen and became a missionary of the Brāhma Samāj. Following the pointing finger of Sen he became interested in Christ and was baptised, later joining the Roman Catholic

Church, to which he continued to own a somewhat troubled allegiance till his death.

From Sen, whose true spiritual successor he was, Upadhyaya inherited a deep devotion to Christ, and a passionate conviction that India had just as much right to the Christian faith as Europe – and to its own interpretation of that faith. We have already seen what he thought about the hard western 'coating' of the Church. He made a careful study of Roman Catholic doctrine, especially of the teaching of Thomas Aquinas, and was much impressed by the coherence of his system, with its firm philosophical grounding in Aristotle. Could not something similar be done for India, he asked. India has many philosophical systems, but the one which is usually regarded as the highest is that of Shankara, known as *advaita* Vedanta, and, greatly daring, Upadhyaya decided to make this the philosophical vehicle for his exposition of the Christian faith. What he attempted was perhaps not unlike what John attempted when he wrote the prologue to the Fourth Gospel. Many Hindus were prepared to grant Christianity a certain validity at the level of a personal, devotional, theistic religion, with a personal God, revealed in an incarnation or *avatāra*. But for themselves, God was higher than that: he was the unconditioned, absolute *Brahman*. 'If *Brahman* is the highest,' thought Upadhyaya, 'then it is *Brahman* whom I proclaim to you. But you do not know his full meaning. You call him *Sat*, *Cit*, *Ānanda*, without knowing the real significance of those terms. I can tell you, for *Saccidānanda* can be understood fully only in terms of the Christian Trinity.' And then he goes on to expound the doctrine of the Trinity, not only in theological statements but also in a magnificent Sanskrit hymn, which has recently become widely popular.

Let me give another example of Upadhyaya's thought – a rather difficult one. The followers of Shankara say that *Brahman* alone is real, and that everything else – including ourselves and the world – is *māyā* or illusion. (Before we criticise that too readily let us recollect that we often think in similar terms; my parents' generation used to describe a committed Christian by saying, 'He has the real thing,' and I think that statement represents a valuable truth. Paul uses the same kind of Platonic language in 2 Cor. 4. 18 when he says: 'The things that are seen are temporal, but the things that are unseen are eternal.') What, then, is the relation of God to the created world? God, or *Brahman*, is *Sat* (Being), and everything else is *asat*, non-being. *Asat*, however, really means that which – unlike God – has no necessary existence; it is what Aquinas calls 'contingent being', as opposed to God's necessary being. And *māyā* is not mere illusion, but is rather 'the fecund divine power' (*Śakti*) which gives birth to multiplicity. If, then, we want to demonstrate to an *advaitin* what Christians mean by creation *ex nihilo* we can explain it by saying that God by his divine power brings contingent being to light out of the nothingness of non-being. This world has only a contingent or relative reality, yet by union with God in Christ we can penetrate to 'the real thing', for only in the contemplation of God's essence – *Sat* itself – is final bliss to be found. Upadhyaya's achievement here is to express the Thomist doctrine of contingent being in Vedantic terminology. He does not, however, advance beyond what Aquinas was trying to express.

Brahmabandhab Upadhyaya was a stormy political figure, and he died in 1907 while awaiting trial on a charge of sedition against the British government. There is no doubt, however, that he was one of the most powerful and original thinkers who has tackled the problem of expressing the Christian faith in Indian terms. Despite the fact that his relations with the Roman hierarchy were uneasy he usually tried to ensure that his formulations did not conflict with Tridentine orthodoxy, and this is a pity; one feels that if his great powers had been used to express a more biblical and less Thomistic faith his contribution would have been even greater. But he was a great man, by any reckoning.

### A. J. Appasamy (b. 1891) – bhakti mārga

A. J. Appasamy, who was formerly bishop of a diocese of the Church of South India and now lives in retirement, was born into a Christian family. As a young man he committed himself to Christ through the work of a well-known missionary (of the Children's Special Service Mission), R. T. Archibald, and later studied at Oxford, where he wrote a thesis comparing the mysticism of St John's Gospel with that of the *bhakti* poets of his native Tamilnad. He had many interesting friends – Sadhu Sundar Singh, the Indian evangelist and mystic who was such a well-known figure in the 1920s; Baron von Hügel, the Roman Catholic mystic; B. H. Streeter, and others. His studies led him to the conclusion – which was reached also by Rudolf Otto in his book *Christianity and the Indian Religion of Grace* (1929) – that the way of *bhakti* was the closest Indian approach to the Christian faith, and that it would be the best vehicle for an Indian theology. Let us look at one or two of his points.

First, unlike Upadhyaya and the *jñāna mārga*, he accepts the idea of incarnation, and is prepared, with safeguards, to use the Hindu word *avatāra*, which literally means 'one who comes down'. In Hindu thought the personal God Vishnu becomes incarnate from time to time – as Krishna, Rama, etc. – in order to save the world in moments of crisis. Obviously Appasamy rejects that view. God has become incarnate only once, in Jesus. Yet the word *avatāra* may, he feels, be used, and indeed it is frequently used in Christian circles in India to describe the incarnation of the Son of God in Jesus.

Secondly, what does Appasamy understand by *mokṣa*? For him this is a very good term to describe what is meant by Jesus' words, 'Abide in me', or Paul's description of the life in Christ. Through faith and loving self-surrender we are united with Christ, yet it is a union in which we are not absorbed; the believer and his Lord retain their distinct personalities. It is no identity we want but loving communion. In the words of a lyric of Rabindranath Tagore, which Appasamy quotes, 'What is the use of salvation if it means absorption? I like eating sugar, but I have no wish to become sugar'.[7]

Another interesting feature of Appasamy's theology is his treatment of the relationship of God to the world – always one

[7] A. J. Appasamy, *What is Moksa?* (Madras, 1931), p. 91.

of the most debated subjects in Indian philosophy. Shankara denies all reality to the world, saying that it is merely *māyā* and that only *Brahman* is real. Ramanuja, however, does give a certain reality to the world, by saying that it is related to God as body is to soul; the world is the body of God. Appasamy gives a Christian interpretation of this: God is not identical with the world, nor is the world mere illusion; rather God is present and active in the world as Logos, using the world as his instrument. He writes, 'There is a Mind or Reason behind the whole world. . . . It is not identical with the world; it is different from the world; but the world lives because of its functioning. . . . Underlying all that we see is the operation of this invisible Personal Power.'[8] Appasamy now goes further, and extends the use of what we may call this Ramanujan analogy to three further contexts – the Person of Christ (Christology), the nature of the Church, and the nature of the presence of Christ at the Lord's Supper. In doing so he approaches rather closely to what some western theologians, notably Professor T. F. Torrance, have done in applying the 'Christological analogy', or what Professor J. McIntyre calls 'the two nature model' in similar contexts.[9] In the Christological context Appasamy writes, 'God took, as it were, a second body, the fleshly organism of Jesus. . . . God revealed himself to men through the human body of Jesus.'[10] Instead of the time-honoured terms of western Christological controversy, which mean little in India, Appasamy here uses the Ramanujan analogy to show that Christ is a single personality, a union of body and soul, with a fully human, created body, yet within whom God dwells as the 'inner controller' or *antaryāmin*. So too in the eucharist the living, spiritual Lord takes the bodily elements of bread and wine, using them and controlling them so that they become channels of his grace. We may or may not think that this body–soul analogy helps us to solve our theo-

[8] *Ibid.*, p. 168.
[9] T. F. Torrance, *Conflict and Agreement in the Church*, i (1959), 230ff. John McIntyre, *The Shape of Christology* (1966), pp. 82ff. See below, pp. 88ff.
[10] A. J. Appasamy, *The Gospel and India's Heritage* (1942), p. 207.

logical problems. It is, however, a very interesting and helpful attempt to explain these problems without recourse to western-'models' and terms.

### Karma mārga

The third traditional Hindu 'way' is the way of action, *karma*. This can perhaps be described as a way of 'works', and the 'works' can be of two kinds – good deeds, and ritual obedience. Traditionally this is the lowest of the ways, the way followed by very ordinary people with no scholarly or mystical talents. It has, however, been given a new interpretation by Mahatma Gandhi, who was happy to describe himself as a follower of the *karma mārga*.[11] He held that our action must be absolutely selfless; we must do good without expecting any reward – his word was *anāsakti*, the renunciation of the fruit of our actions – and if we do that we find that this kind of non-violent, utterly selfless service of God and humanity is the supreme way of self-realisation. And Gandhi was, of course, a magnificent example of his own teaching. He really transformed the whole idea of *karma mārga*, taking it out of the realm of petty piety, and transforming it into the ideal of loving, non-violent service.

It is strange that so far no great Indian Christian theologian has followed up this line and given a thoroughgoing Christian exposition of the *karma mārga*. One or two men like J. C. Kumarappa and S. K. George have gone some of the way, but they – perhaps rightly – were more taken up in their Gandhian activities than in any theological task. I am inclined to think that the man who has most convincingly followed the *karma mārga* in recent days was one who was neither Indian nor European, but Dr Martin Luther King, a trained theologian who was also a convinced Gandhian, and who put into costly action the principle of loving, non-violent service. The recent writings of M. M. Thomas, especially perhaps his book *Salvation and Humanisation* (1971), indicate the possibility of a new and challenging interpretation of *karma mārga* in terms of

[11] N. Minz, *Mahatma Gandhi and Hindu–Christian Dialogue*, pp. 29 and 143.

Christian involvement in the Asian revolution, and in man's struggle for justice, peace and true humanity; for, as Thomas says, 'Humanisation is inherent in the message of salvation in Christ.'[12]

## P. Chenchiah (1886–1959)

We have been looking at the three traditional *mārgas*, and at Christian reinterpretations of them. Not all Hindu thinkers, however, are content to remain within the confines of the traditional systems, and one of the greatest, and most influential modern Indian thinkers has been Sri Aurobindo (1872–1950), the Bengali political leader who gave up politics and retired to an *ashram* at Pondicherry, and who today has many enthusiastic followers in the western world. His teaching was a combination of western evolutionary science and Indian mysticism, and his views have much in common with the creative evolution of Bergson, and with the more recent writing of Teilhard de Chardin. P. Chenchiah was a layman who became a Christian while studying in Madras Christian College, and who in a series of brilliant and exuberant articles in various periodicals outlined an approach which has been characterised as 'the new creation' theology.

Its basis is really 2 Cor. 5. 17, 'If any man is in Christ he is a new creation.' That had been Chenchiah's own experience; his life had been transformed when he accepted Christ, and he was convinced that this new creation was something infectious, which could spread and change whole societies and the whole world. The essential thing was direct encounter with Christ—what Indian thinkers call *pratyakṣa anubhava*. Aurobindo, unlike most Hindu thinkers who look to the *ātman* within, believed that it was possible to receive divine and transforming power from outside oneself, and that those who are thus transformed can help to transform the world. Chenchiah seized on this idea, interpreting it in terms of faith-union with Christ

---

[12] M. M. Thomas, *Salvation and Humanisation*, p. 10. For a fuller treatment of Thomas as representative of a Christian *karma mārga*, see R. H. S. Boyd, *Introduction to Indian Christian Theology* (2nd edn, Madras, 1974), chap. XVI.

and the power of the Holy Spirit. Christ is the first-fruits of the new creation, and those who are 'in' him participate in a totally new kind of humanity. Here are some short quotations which give some idea of the heady language he uses:

Jesus is the *adi-purusha* (original man) of a new creation. . . . In Jesus, creation mounts a step higher. . . . Jesus is the origin of the species of the sons of God.[13]

I feel the two great urges of Indian Christians are a desire for direct contact with Jesus (*pratyaksa*) and an aspiration for rebirth – to be born a son of God in the image of Jesus. . . .

True evangelism consists in reproducing Jesus. The Indian Christian should harness the Holy Spirit to the creation of new life.[14]

The Holy Spirit is the new cosmic energy; the Kingdom of God the new order; the children of God the new type that Christ has inaugurated. The Gospel is that God in Jesus has made a new creation. . . . The children of God are the next step in evolution and the Kingdom of God the next stage in cosmos.[15]

In Chenchiah we see what has been called a 'double synthesis'; he is seeking to express his Christian faith in the context both of Hindu spirituality and of western scientific – and particularly evolutionary – thought. Today his writings sound rather dated in some ways; and yet a great deal of what he says is very close to Teilhard, though expressed in largely Indian idiom.

One of Chenchiah's favourite expressions was 'the raw fact of Christ'. He once wrote, 'We accept nothing as obligatory save Christ. Church doctrine and dogma, whether from the west or from the past, whether from apostles or from modern critics, are to be tested before they are accepted.'[16] But we have to ask ourselves whether we can in fact avoid doctrine; can we really

---

[13] Quoted in *National Christian Council Review* (1943), p. 363.
[14] *Guardian* (Madras), 6 Feb 1947, and *S. India Churchman*, Oct. 1960.
[15] *Rethinking Christianity in India* (Madras, 1938), p. 57.
[16] *Ibid.* p. 150.

put ourselves in the position of the first disciples who had a saving encounter with Christ, but needed no doctrinal formulations? That is one of the questions which concern us in this book.

We have looked at a number of 'types of Indian theology' (to use H. R. Mackintosh's phrase), and seen how their exponents attempt to grapple with the problem of expressing the Christian faith in India. Some, like Goreh and Upadhyaya, were deeply conscious of the western models they were trying to reproduce in Indian shape; others, like Chenchiah, were chiefly anxious to discard everything except the 'original stimulus' of Jesus. Kaj Baago has written that 'the day when a religion crosses the boundaries of its native soil and moves into another cultural sphere is among the most fateful in its history'. Indigenisation, he believes, is not just a matter of Indian church architecture or sitting on the floor:

Real indigenisation means crossing the borderline . . . and moving into another religion, another culture, taking only Christ with oneself. Indigenisation is evangelisation. It is the planting of the Gospel inside another culture, another philosophy and another religion.[17]

Is that so? Or must we impose prefabricated safeguards on the message? That will be the subject of the next chapter.

[17] K. Baago, *Pioneers of Indian Christianity* (Bangalore, 1969), p. 85.

# 3

## DEFENDERS OF THE FAITH –
## THE 'SUBORDINATE STANDARDS'

### *Safeguarding the faith*

The missionaries came to India, they preached, they translated and circulated the Scriptures, they disputed, they counselled. People listened and reacted; some mocked, others stayed to hear more, and some accepted Christ and were bold enough to receive baptism. And so the Church took root. One of the earliest theological writings of which we have record in Gujarat was a catechism, prepared in Surat by the Armenian Baptist missionary C. C. Aratoon, and taken with him to Carey at Serampore for printing when he left Gujarat in 1818. This was no doubt a catechism for enquirers. It was only later on, after the Church had become firmly established and organised, and especially after the commencement of theological training for future ministers, that the missionaries decided that vernacular versions of the reformed confessions were required. The Anglican missionaries had, of course, translated the Apostles' and Nicene Creeds at a very early stage, as part of the translation of the liturgy.

The Presbytery of Kathiawar and Gujarat – then a presbytery of the Presbyterian Church in Ireland – drew up its first course of theological study in 1864 for a Brāhmin convert, Chaganlal Bhagwandas. This was a private course, but in 1878 a regular theological class was begun in Ahmedabad, and it is significant that in that year the scholarly Joseph van Someren Taylor produced a translation of the Westminster Shorter Catechism, a translation which is still in use, and is quite a valuable source of theological terminology. Taylor, originally a London Missionary Society missionary who had been born in India and had an unrivalled knowledge of Gujarati – he is still known as 'the father of Gujarati grammar' – was a very wise man. I remember years ago turning up question 3 in the catechism to find how he had translated the difficult word 'person' in 'How many persons are there in the Godhead?' – only to find that he had avoided the word altogether, translating as 'there are three in the Godhead. . . .' The word, however, cannot always be so neatly avoided!

An interesting sidelight on Church history is that there was in fact an earlier Gujarati translation of the catechism, made in the 1860s, by no less a person than Robert Young of Concordance fame, who was then Superintendent of the Surat Mission Press. It is said that Young – no doubt as a scholarly exercise – translated the catechism into about fifteen languages, including Greek and Hebrew! The Gujarati version which survives, however, is Taylor's. Later, Taylor translated the Westminster Confession, and this appeared in print – complete with Scripture proofs – in 1889, an edition which remained in use until superseded by that of W. G. Mulligan, published as recently as 1949.

Those events in Gujarat give us a clear idea of how Protestant missionaries sought to ensure that the young Church in India should remain faithful to the 'subordinate standards' of the reformed tradition. For the Roman Catholic Church, there was, presumably, no problem, as the monolithic structure of the world-wide Church ensures that the Roman *magisterium* is in control, and questions of doctrine arising from any quarter can be settled only there. To begin with, most Protestant Churches in India were regarded as 'branches' of their European or American 'mother Churches' (a phrase still heard surprisingly frequently in India!), and indeed one of the largest Protestant Churches in India, the Methodist Church in Southern Asia, is still integrally related to the United Methodist Church of the USA. I shall speak for the moment only for the Presbyterian tradition, but the description will apply, *mutatis mutandis*, to many of the Protestant traditions in India.

In Gujarat, then, from 1842 until 1900 there was a presbytery of the Irish Presbyterian Church. From 1904 till 1924 the presbytery belonged to the Presbyterian Church of India. In 1924 there was a union with the Congregationalists to form the United Church of Northern India, which in 1970 passed into the new Church of North India. Thus from 1842 until 1924 the Westminster Confession was the subordinate standard of the Church. The UCNI after 1924 drew up its own fairly brief 'Confession of Faith', subscription to which was obligatory on ministers, though it did not entirely supersede the Westminster Confession as a teaching standard. We may say, then, that for well over a hundred years, and at a decisive formative stage in the life of the Church, the Westminster Confession was its subordinate standard.

### *An Indian view of the Westminster Confession*

Let us try, therefore, to look at the Confession with Indian eyes as it were, not in order to test its orthodoxy, but to see how its language and phraseology speak to the Indian situation. First, we should recall briefly the circumstances which brought it into being in 1646. The Westminster Assembly of Divines was composed mainly of episcopally ordained clergymen of the Church of England, with the assistance of Scottish assessors, in order to prepare a scheme for uniformity of doctrine, worship and Church government, according to the Presbyterian pattern, for the newly united kingdom of England and Scotland.[1] It is, therefore, a document drawn up at a specific time and with a specific purpose, intended not merely to state a minimum of Christian belief (like the Apostles' Creed), but to rule out various types of error in doctrine and Church government, especially these connected with the Roman Church and with episcopacy. It should also be remembered that the Assembly was called into being by Parliament in 1643, and was therefore very closely connected with government – a sort of Presbyterian manifestation of Caesaropapism, so to say. Nothing could have

[1] George S. Hendry, *The Westminster Confession for Today* (1960), pp. 9, 10.

been further from the minds of the divines than the thought that one day their document would be the doctrinal standard of an Indian Church independent of European control, living under a secular state and surrounded by Hindus!

So let us look at some of the statements of the Confession, and ask ourselves how they sound in an Indian context.

### The Trinity (II. 3)

In the unity of the Godhead there be three persons, of one substance, power and eternity; God the Father, God the Son, and God the Holy Ghost. The Father is of none, neither begotten nor proceeding; the Son is eternally begotten of the Father; the Holy Ghost eternally proceeding from the Father and the Son.

There are at least four difficult technical terms here – person, substance, begotten and proceeding – three of them derived from Latin. The word 'person' cannot be translated directly from English into, say, Gujarati, for in common parlance 'person' means 'individual', and that is precisely what it does not mean in this context. 'Substance' also is a difficult word, implying something solid and material; one has to go back beyond the Latin *substantia* to the Greek *ousia*. Then the word 'begotten' – admittedly not Latin. Any translation into Gujarati would imply a sexual relationship, and would cause misunderstanding to a Hindu and scandal to a Muslim. 'Proceeding' is a neutral sort of word; it is a Scriptural word too – if by Scriptural we mean that it is found in the Vulgate (John 15. 26). But will a literal translation bring out its real meaning? Obviously the task which Joseph Taylor and Graham Mulligan undertook in translating the Confession was no easy one!

### Original sin (VI. 3)

. . . They being the root of all mankind, the guilt of this sin was imputed, and the same death in sin and corrupted nature conveyed to all their posterity, descending from them by ordinary generation.

On the whole it is true to say that Hindus have comparatively little consciousness of sin; they are much more burdened by the weight of *karma* – the fruit of actions bad and good and the belief that one has to atone for one's sins through repeated incarnations – than by anxiety about sin. Swami Vivekananda, for example, said that it was a sin to call a man a sinner. It is, therefore, important that the Christian teaching on the nature of sin should be clearly stated. Hinduism holds that each soul lives as it were in a closed circuit, and is responsible for its own deeds alone; there can be no idea of solidarity in guilt, nor transmission of guilt from one person to another. The Confession makes two statements here: one that the guilt of Adam's sin is imputed to all mankind through their solidarity with him ('the root'), and the other that corruption is conveyed or transmitted to all his descendants who are born through the union of the sexes (i.e. excluding Christ who was born of a Virgin). We make no judgment here on the theology underlying the Confession at this point, but simply note the Latin word 'impute', again taken from the Vulgate (e.g. Rom. 5. 13). The point about conveyance of corruption to all posterity descended by ordinary generation is of course a piece of Augustine's teaching, and tends to confirm a commonly held Hindu belief that the source of all sin is in the body and its passions, and that the road to virtue consists in asceticism.

## The covenant (vii. 6)

. . . Under the Gospel, when Christ the substance was exhibited, the ordinances in which this covenant is dispensed are the preaching of the Word and the administration of the sacraments. . . .

A comparison is being made here between the covenant under the law and under the Gospel. Under the law it was administered by promises, prophecies and 'types' – i.e. types of Christ – but under the Gospel Christ himself, the 'substance' or 'antitype', has appeared. It is significant that in the interests of clarity the Latin text of the Confession actually adds the word 'antitype' – 'exhibito iam Christo, substantia scilicet ac antitypo'. The proof-text quoted here is Col. 2. 17, 'Which are a shadow of things to come; but the body is of Christ.' The point of difficulty here for an Indian reader is that this is a piece of Platonism, and implies an understanding of the doctrine of ideas, and the theory of typology.

### Christology (VIII. 2)

... So that two whole, perfect, and distinct natures, the Godhead and the manhood, were inseparably joined together in one person, without conversion, composition, or confusion. Which person is very God and very man, yet one Christ, the only Mediator between God and man.

Here we have a clear statement of the orthodox Christology of the Council of Chalcedon, A.D. 451, which can be summarised in the phrase 'two natures in one person'. The English words come straight from the Latin *natura* and *persona*, but these are quite a long way from the Greek *phusis* and *hupostasis*. The three adverbial phrases are slightly different from the four Greek adverbs of Chalcedon, but we may take it that the first and third rule out Eutychean monophysitism and the second the possibility of a Nestorian dualism. In a later chapter we shall be looking more closely at some of this terminology; here we may simply draw attention to the great difficulty, or rather the impossibility, of finding a Sanskritic equivalent of *hupostasis/persona*.

### The mediator (VIII. 5)

The Lord Jesus, by his perfect obedience and sacrifice of himself, which he through the eternal Spirit once offered up unto God, hath fully satisfied the justice of the Father. . . .

None of the proof-texts suggested here mentions the idea of the satisfaction of the Father's justice, and in fact the word 'satisfy' is not used in this sense in the Bible. As is well known, this usage was developed by Anselm. It is a purely Latin usage, and has as its background medieval and feudal ideas of the infringement of a person's honour and its satisfaction by paying a suitable penalty. However, it is admittedly an idea which is not at all unfamiliar in India, so whatever our theological judgment, we need not reject it on linguistic or sociological grounds.

## The fate of non-Christians (x. 4)

. . . Much less can men not professing the Christian religion be saved in any other way whatsoever, be they ever so diligent to frame their lives according to the light of nature, and the law of that religion they do profess; and to assert and maintain that they may, is very pernicious and to be detested.

The Confession is here speaking of the fate of the non-elect, and goes on to condemn virtually all non-Christians. There is, however, an inconsistency between this and para. 3 of the same chapter, which says that regeneration and salvation are extended to 'all other elect persons, who are incapable of being outwardly called by the ministry of the word'. From this it would appear that it does not matter what one's religion is provided one is numbered among the elect. We shall refrain once more from passing theological judgment, but we cannot avoid saying that this paragraph could scarcely be said to be an encouragement to missionary witness!

## Justification (xi. 1)

Those whom God effectually calleth he also freely justifieth.

The point I wish to make here is a familiar one – the inadequacy of the Latin *justificāre*, and hence the English 'justify' – as a translation of the Greek *dikaioun*, since the force of the verbal part of the Latin compound is 'to *make* righteous'. This is another term whose translation into the Sanskritic languages raises great difficulties. The word used in the present Gujarati Bible, *nyāyikaraṇa*, is a literal translation of the Latin, meaning 'making just', but it is virtually meaningless to non-Christians. The new Roman Catholic translation, which means 'to make meritorious' (*puṇyaśālī*), is if anything worse. A rather better phrase which has been suggested is 'to make free from guilt' (*doṣamukta*) or 'to acquit'; but here we enter the realm of exegesis rather than translation – a process which, by the way, is often necessary in transposing theological ideas from one language to another.

### Repentance (xv)

Here we can have nothing but praise for the excellent opening sentence of the Westminster divines:

Repentance unto life is an evangelical grace, the doctrine whereof is to be preached by every minister of the gospel, as well as that of faith in Christ.

It is simply to the word 'repentance' itself that we must draw attention, since it is connected with the Latin *paenitentia* or penitence, and so with *poena*, punishment. We naturally begin to think immediately of the pre-Reformation Roman teaching on penance, indulgences and all the rest. It is unfortunate that the English word has been taken from the Latin one which comes in the Vulgate – *paenitentia* – for of course the meaning of the Greek, *metanoia*, is quite different, and signifies 'change of mind' or even 'change of heart', as the *nous* could be regarded as the seat of the whole personality. Whoever prepared the Latin translation of the Confession was aware of this difficulty, for instead of *paenitentia* it uses the rather rare word *resipiscentia* – which is, indeed, found in Lactantius (d. 325) as a translation of *metanoia*.

The unfortunate thing for India here is that there *are* words which are very close translations of *paenitentia*, and in the current Gujarati translation of the Bible, for example, it is these words, *pastāvo* and *paścāttāp*, which have been used, with misleading results. The word used in the new translations, both Protestant and Roman Catholic, is *hriday-palṭo*, which means 'change of heart', and is therefore much closer to *metanoia* – and to what the whole matter is about.

### The civil magistrate (xxiii)

The civil magistrate . . . hath authority, and it is his duty, to take order, that unity and peace be preserved in the Church, that the truth of God be kept pure and entire, that all blasphemies and heresies be suppressed. . . . For the better effecting whereof, he hath power to call synods, be present at them, and to provide that whatsoever be transacted in them be according to the mind of God.

It is not necessary to say much about this chapter, as it has long been queried, qualified or rejected by the various Presbyterian Churches. It springs from the tradition of Caesaropapism, which Calvin sought to perpetuate in Geneva, Knox in Scotland, and Henry VIII in England. The sentiments expressed sound distinctly odd, however, in India, which is a secular state, and where the well-being of the Church depends on the continuance of the secular state and its renunciation of all temporal claims over the Church. In the old days all British coins bore the legend 'FID. DEF., IND. IMP.' – a silent memorial to Henry VIII, Queen Victoria and Disraeli. 'IND. IMP.' has gone since 1947. Indian Christians, studying the latest coinage of their British friends, would perhaps place a question mark against 'FID. DEF.' and the theocratic state which it presupposes.

## Monistic mysticism (XXVI. 3)

. . . This communion which the saints have with Christ doth not make them in any wise partakers of the substance of his Godhead, or to be equal with Christ in any respect: either of which to affirm is impious and blasphemous.

This very interesting little paragraph is the only one in the whole Confession which indicates that the Westminster divines may have been aware of some features of Indian religion. They may, of course, have had Greek ideas of 'divinisation' in mind, or possibly the views of some of the European mystics like Eckhart or Thomas Münzer. What they say agrees with Appasamy's view of personal mysticism, and Tagore's dictum about liking sugar but not wishing to become sugar.

## The Lord's Supper (XXIX)

This important chapter is largely devoted to the repudiation of three erroneous doctrines – the sacrifice of the mass; the doctrine of transubstantiation; and Luther's teaching on consubstantiation. The sections therefore presuppose an understanding of these Reformation controversies, and also of Aristotle's teaching on substance and accidents, as interpreted by Aquinas. They make one realise how much eucharistic instruction is based on the refutation of erroneous teaching rather than on a positive presentation. For a young Church, is it not possible to pass beyond old controversies to a new, yet faithful, exegesis?

### A meaningful symbol in its context

With our western historical and cultural background it is possible for us to understand the Confession, and appreciate the great principles which it enshrines. There are some sections about which many would have certain reservations – double predestination, the positive identification of antichrist (xxv. 6), the chapter on the civil magistrate, for example. In a number of Presbyterian Churches those reservations and questions have found expression in General Assembly debates and legislation on 'Articles Declaratory'[2]. Yet viewing it as a whole there is no doubt that the Westminster Confession is a massive, impressive and, I believe, valid description of the body of Christian truth. It is couched in the idiom of the seventeenth century, and its language and terminology go back not only to the Scriptures (as was the chief concern of the Westminster divines) but also to the Greek and Latin Fathers, and to the pre-Reformation Church of the middle ages. Its structure, as a *Summa* of Christian doctrine, is based on Calvin, who in turn owes a great deal to medieval as well as Patristic classical theology. There is no doubt, however, that this Confession – like many others such as the Scots Confession of 1560 or the Heidelberg Catechism – points us towards the Truth, the Reality of God's dealings with mankind. Through all its limitations we see looming something of the shape and structure of God's activity as it is revealed to us in the Bible.

[2] See, e.g., *Reports of the General Assembly of the Presbyterian Church in Ireland* (1971), pp. 12–17.

## A 'subordinate' standard

We must never forget, however, that the Confession is a *subordinate* standard, which points us very clearly to the supreme standard of the Scriptures. The importance of this point is indicated by the fact that the chapter on Scripture comes first in the Confession. As George Hendry says, 'The central principle of the Reformed faith . . . is that the Word of God is the only infallible rule of faith and practice, and no other document can be regarded in the same light.'[3] The Reformers were rebelling against the idea that the dogmas of the Roman Church were divinely revealed and therefore infallible. Their attitude to all 'decrees of councils, opinions of ancient writers, doctrines of men' (.1 10) is that they are fallible, and come under the judgment of 'the supreme Judge', and that supreme Judge is 'the Holy Spirit speaking in Scripture'. There is no doubt at all that the Westminster divines would have included their own Confession among those 'doctrines of men' which fall under the judgment of Scripture, and would have been the first to resist any attempt – above all any attempt with the aid of the civil authority – to give to their document an infallibility and immutability which can be accorded only to the Word of God. Not long ago I listened to Dr Hans Küng speaking on the subject of infallibility to a large mixed audience of Protestants and Roman Catholics.[4] The Protestant part of the audience listened with great satisfaction while he demolished the claims of his own Roman Church to infallibility. They were perhaps not quite so happy when he turned his guns on them, and criticised them for sometimes having an attitude towards their confessions which was little different from the Roman attitude to officially pronounced dogmas. He then spoke, in a manner reminiscent of Luther, of the 'decisiveness' of Christ and the Scriptures. That is, indeed, good reformed teaching. We should never be afraid to question the Confession, and to judge it, as

[3] Hendry, *op. cit.*, p. 11.
[4] Lecture at Melbourne University, 17 August 1971.

every doctrine must be judged, in the light of Scripture, and of the Lord of Scripture.

## India and the reformed confessions

The question now arises: for an Indian Christian to be 'ortho-dox' is it necessary for him to assent to the faith in *this* form – the form of one of the reformed confessions? Until comparatively recently subscription to the Westminster Confession *was* required of all ministers and elders in what was originally the Presbyterian Church in Gujarat. What is the position now, for example, in the newly formed Church of North India, which unites Anglicans (now sitting rather lightly to the 39 Articles), Methodists (of the British and Australian connection), who presumably are guided by the Sermons of John Wesley, and members of the Church of the Brethren who maintain that the Bible is their *only* creed, and that no man-made creed or confession is binding on them? Let us look briefly at what the *Plan of Union* says in the chapter entitled *The Doctrines of the Church* (chap. IV, pp. 4–6).

The CNI gives its own brief statement of belief in three ar-ticles. First, it identifies itself with the faith of the universal Church:

The CNI holds the faith which the Church has ever held in Jesus Christ the Redeemer of the world, in whom alone men are saved by grace through faith, and in accordance with the revelation of God which He made, being Himself God Incarnate, it worships one God, Father, Son and Holy Spirit.

That sentence states, without defining, the doctrines of the di-vinity of Christ, the Trinity, and salvation by grace through faith.

Secondly comes a strongly reformed statement on the Scriptures: The CNI

accepts the Holy Scriptures of the Old Testament and the New Testament as the inspired Word of God, as containing all things necessary to salvation, and as the supreme and decisive standard of faith, and acknowledges that the Church must always be ready to correct and reform itself in accordance with the teaching of those Scriptures as the Holy Spirit shall reveal it.

Thirdly, the Apostles' and Nicene Creeds are accepted 'as witnessing to and guarding that faith'.

That is a kind of minimal statement for the present. As regards the past, the CNI (IV. 5)

acknowledges the witness to the Catholic faith contained in the Confessions of Faith adopted both at the time of the Reformation and subsequently, and formulated by the uniting Churches or their parent Churches.

It goes on to say that such

traditional declarations of faith, generally used for the instruction of the faithful in any of the uniting Churches, may continue to be so used after the Union, so long as they are consistent with the doctrinal standards officially set forth by the CNI.

The Westminster Confession is included among such declarations of faith.

What of the future? The way is open for new developments here. The *Plan* says (IV. 5),

For the confession of its faith before the world and for the guidance of its teachers and the edification of the faithful, it shall be competent for the CNI to issue its own statements, provided always that such statements are agreeable to the Holy Scriptures.

The Church in India has perhaps not yet reached the point at which it can begin to draw up its own Confession. Yet events are moving in that direction, and the foundations are being laid in theological thinking. I am reminded of the title of an interesting series of books which present the teaching of a wide variety of Indian theologians; the title is 'Confessing the Faith in India'.[5] The day will come when Indian Christian divines will draw up their Confession which will speak to the needs of

---

[5] 'Confessing the Faith in India' – a series published by the Christian Institute for the Study of Religion and Society, Bangalore, and the Christian Literature Society, Madras.

the Church in India as surely as the Westminster Confession did to the Church of the seventeenth century.

That task will involve much study of how Christian doctrinal formulations first emerge, in any culture. And in our next chapter we shall consider how systematic doctrine first began to be hammered out in the evangelism and the controversies of the early Church.

# 4

# THE WESTERN ORIGINS OF
# THEOLOGICAL FORMULATION

In the last chapter we examined a typical post-Reformation confession – that formulated by the Westminster divines – in the light of an Indian lamp, as it were, and discovered that it contains many words, phrases and ideas which reflect not merely the witness of the New Testament, but a post-New Testament, a Graeco-Roman or a medieval background of thought and culture. Beyond one small and not altogether explicit paragraph, there was nothing to indicate that the Westminster divines were conscious of the vast world of Indian culture in which already, in their time, the Church had been established for well over a thousand years. The Reformation and post-Reformation confessions are all uncompromisingly 'western'.

Here we must pause for a moment to clarify our own terminology. European theologians usually employ the words 'eastern' and 'western' to signify 'Greek' and 'Latin' (or Roman) respectively; the Eastern Churches are those which never adopted the Latin language, and which eventually threw off their allegiance to Rome and became a group of autonomous Churches, with liturgies in Syriac or Greek, and later in Russian and various other languages. In this sense 'eastern' theology or 'spirituality' refers to the group of Syrian, Greek and Russian Churches. From the point of view of India, however, 'western' includes not only the Latin but the Greek heritage; modern western civilisation is clearly seen as continuous with the Graeco-Roman culture, and therefore any features of civilisation, or of ecclesiastical thought or life which are linked with Greek philosophy or Greek institutions, are thought of as western. In what follows, therefore, as in the title of this chapter, I shall use the word 'western' to mean Graeco-Roman. When we wish to define more closely we shall distinguish between 'Greek' and 'Latin' elements within that western tradition.

### How did systematic theology arise?

We come now to a rather basic question. Why did it become necessary for the Church to begin defining its beliefs? We have already mentioned the fact that the Church of the Brethren, one of the six constituent Churches of the Church of North India, has traditionally maintained that the Bible is its only creed, and that further man-made formulations are unnecessary. If that is so, why did the early Church ever begin formulating its beliefs? And *how* did it carry out that task at the beginning?

There were two major factors behind the earliest formulation of doctrine: first, the needs of proclamation, and secondly the need to refute heresy.

As C. H. Dodd has pointed out in *The Apostolic Preaching and its Development*, we find a definite series of points in the five proclamatory sermons of Peter recorded in Acts. The main emphases of this primitive *kerugma* are the following: the age of fulfilment has dawned; this has taken place through the life, death and resurrection of Jesus; through his resurrection Jesus has been exalted; the Holy Spirit has been poured out on the Church as the sign of Christ's power; Christ will one day – probably soon – return in glory; God's offer to all men who repent is forgiveness, salvation and the gift of the Holy Spirit.[1] In Rom. 10. 8–9, Paul gives a brief summary of 'the word of faith which we proclaim'. It reads, 'If you confess with your mouth that Jesus is Lord, and believe in your heart that God raised Him from the dead, you shall be saved.' It has often

---

[1] Summarised by Alan Richardson in *Theological Wordbook of the Bible* (1963), *s.v.* PREACH.

been pointed out that the words 'Jesus is Lord' were probably the first Christian creed, and that they may well have been the earliest baptismal creed of the Church (cf. also Phil. 2. 11). Gradually, however, more detailed summaries of the Christian faith were elaborated, and used as baptismal creeds for new Christians.

It was, however, the task of defending the beliefs of the Church against heretical teaching which gave rise to that more detailed analysis of the articles of belief which we associate with dogmatic theology – the effort not merely to state a belief but to explain something of its inner meaning. We see this process at work already in the New Testament, for example in the refutation of gnostic ideas in Colossians, or of antinomian teaching in 2 Peter and Jude. As soon as this work of refutation and explanation begins, it becomes necessary to use a vocabulary taken from the surrounding cultural environment. When Paul preaching to the Athenians quoted the poet Aratus (Acts 17. 28); when, writing to people in Galatia and Rome who were familiar with both Jewish and Roman law, he spoke of *dikaiosis* – he was working with the principle that the meaning of the faith must be explained in terms current in the cultural environment of the people. The same is true when the fourth evangelist in his Prologue uses the word 'Logos', familiar to Greek Stoics and to Jews of the Philonic tradition. When the author of the epistle to the Hebrews uses apparently Platonic language to describe the law as the shadow and Christ as the reality (e.g. Heb. 10. 1) he is doing the same thing.

J. N. D. Kelly points out how in the Apostolic Fathers (Clement of Rome, 'Barnabas', Ignatius, Hermas) the task of witness gradually becomes merged in interpretation as the Church's 'unconscious theology' begins to develop.[2] But it is in the work of the Apologists, and especially of Justin Martyr that we begin to see most clearly how pre-existent philosophical patterns of thought begin to influence the formulation of Christian doctrine.

[2] J. N. D. Kelly, *Early Christian Doctrines* (1958), p. 90.

## *The Apologists*

The first doctrine whose origins we shall consider is that of the Trinity, or rather at this early stage the question of the relationship between Jesus and God. The Jews believed in *one* God, Father and Creator; how was this monotheistic belief, which was shared by philosophically minded Greeks, to be combined with the new evidence afforded by the New Testament – the story of Jesus, and the claims made for him by his followers? How, in fact, was Jesus the Christ related to God?

To answer this question, the Apologists turned to the most promising philosophical instrument they could use – the Logos-doctrine of the Stoics, which was familiar also to many Jews through the work of Philo. In any case, the term had already been used in John's Gospel; it was simply a matter of explaining – by drawing on the pre-existing philosophical background – the inner meaning of the term.

For the Stoics, the Logos was the divine activity in the world, activating and ordering all that is. They distinguished two aspects of the Logos, *Logos endiathetos* and *Logos prophorikos*, the word immanent or internal and the word expressed or outgoing. The Apologists use this idea in order to explain how Christ is pre-temporally one with the Father, and yet is manifested in the world of space and time.[3] Their solution to the question of Christ's relation to the Father, then, is that as pre-existent, Christ is the Father's *thought*, the unexpressed, immanent Word. As manifested in creation he is the *expression* of that thought in speech. (We may note in passing, that this is a well-known distinction in Indian philosophy – the difference between *avyakta* or unexpressed and *vyakta* or expressed.)

Using this exposition Justin Martyr is able to posit the Son's unity with the Father, while maintaining that the two are distinct in name and in number. The image or 'model' which Justin uses is one that was destined to become very influential: Christ is related to the Father, he says, as a ray of light is to the sun. Clearly the two are co-eternal, and you cannot find one

[3] *Ibid.* p. 96.

without the other; and yet they are distinct in name and number. We shall see later how this 'model' has been taken up by a modern Indian theologian, Dhanjibhai Fakirbhai, and how it goes back also to the Upaniṣads.

Before we leave the Apologists let us note that it was Theophilus of Antioch who first used the word 'Triad' (Greek *Trias*) in connection with God, though for him the Triad was God, his Word and his Wisdom. (Later theology combined word and wisdom as aspects of the Logos or son, and posited the Holy Spirit as the third distinct member of the Triad.)

## *Tertullian (c. 160–223)*

Now let us take a look at the great pioneer figure of Latin theology, Tertullian, who has left an abiding mark on the theology of the Western Church, both in the 'shape' of dogmatic theology (i.e. the selection of doctrines which make up systematic theology and the order in which they are treated) and also in its vocabulary. He has been called the father of Latin Theology and also (by B. B. Warfield, for example) the originator of the doctrine of the Trinity.[4] We shall examine some of his significant contributions to the development of theology.

### *The Rule of Faith*
In *De Praescriptione Haereticorum*, Chap. xiii, Tertullian gives what he calls the *Regula Fidei* – the basic points of doctrine which raise no questions among Christians, and are challenged only by heretics. It is really a short creed, speaking of the one God, the Creator; of creation through his Word; of that Word being called the Son; of the incarnation of the Word in Christ; of his death and resurrection; of the sending of the 'vicarious power' of the Spirit (*vicaria vis*); of the second coming; of the promise of eternal life; and of judgment.

In this 'Rule of Faith' we see a clear outline of what was

---

[4] B. B. Warfield, *Studies in Tertullian and Augustine* (New York, 1930), p. 18.

later to become the order of items in the Creed. For our present examination the stress on the Logos or Word (*verbum*) is significant.

### The word 'Trinity'

Tertullian is the first theologian to use the Latin word *Trinitas* and to use it as we do, not in the way of Theophilus' *Trias*. In *Adv. Praxean* chap. 2 he writes of

the mystery of the *oikonomia* which disposes the unity into *Trinity*, positing three (*tres dirigens*), the Father, the Son and the Holy Spirit; they are three, however, not by separate subsistence (*non statu*), but by their 'grade' (*gradu*); not by substance, but by form (*nec substantia sed forma*).

In that brief reference we find a good many terms that were later moulded into the doctrinal formulations of the Church. Here is the beginning.

### The relation of Father and Son

Tertullian, developing his theology with the use of Latin terminology, carries on the work of the Apologists in his effort to describe the relation of Father and Son. His purpose, especially in the *Apology*, is missionary; but he also has a heretical opponent to refute – the modalistic monarchianism of Praxeas who held the unity of God at the expense of the distinct reality of Son and Spirit. And in order to carry out this double task of proclamation and refutation he uses the philosophical instrument which was already to hand – the Logos-doctrine as interpreted by the Apologists. That is a good example of how dogmatic theology 'grows'.

Following the Apologists, he uses a number of images or 'models' to describe the relationship – fountain and river, root and tree etc. – but it is especially with the model of sun and ray that we are concerned. Like the Apologists he uses the Stoic Logos as his instrument – all the more readily, no doubt, because he had himself at one time been a Stoic, and knew their tradition from within. (We remember that most, though not all of the best Indian Christian theologians are those who are themselves converts from Hinduism.)

When he puts the Stoic distinction of *Logos endiathetos* and *Logos prophorikos* into Latin we get *ratio* for the immanent, unexpressed Logos, and *sermo* or *verbum* for the word expressed. God's *ratio* is with him from the beginning, and it is through this *ratio* or thought, which Tertullian also calls *spirit* (following the Stoic Cleanthes) that God creates the universe. (*Apol.* xxi. 10ff.) When the word of creation is spoken, the Logos is 'brought forth' (*prolatum*), and in virtue of that 'prolation', is called 'begotten' (*generatum*), and so is known as 'Son'.

This spiritualising or philosophising of the idea of the generation of the Son is important. For the Greeks the idea of sons of God born through the union of the sexes was common. Tertullian wishes to make it clear that when the *Logos* is called 'Son of God' nothing of this kind is intended. Those who to-day are familiar with missionary work among Muslims know how important this point is; to say that God has a Son is to imply sexual relations, and no sin is greater than to make such a suggestion.[5]

Tertullian then adds that the Son can himself be called God 'because of the unity of his substance' [sc. with God] (*ex unitate substantiae*). Here for the first time we get the emergence of the Latin word 'substance', which is presumably Tertullian's translation of *hupostasis*, literally the *underlying* ('under-standing') essence of God. And then comes Tertullian's exposition of the sun-and-ray model (xxi. 12):

When a ray comes out from the sun, a part comes out of the whole; yet *the sun is in the ray*, because the ray is 'of' the sun; it is not a case of the *separation* of the substance, but of its *extension*. In the same way spirit comes from spirit, God from God, just as light burning from light. The source of the material (*materiae matrix*) remains complete and unaffected, even though you may take several offshoots (*traduces*) from it: in the same way what goes out from God (*profectum*) is both God and Son of God, and both are one.

[5] Cf. Klaus Klostermaier, *Kristvidya* (Bangalore, 1967), pp. 8–10.

There we see the Latin source of some phrases which have found their way into the Nicene Creed and – through *Adeste fideles*! – into popular piety: *Deus de Deo; Lumen de Lumine.*

It is this *radius Dei*, the ray of light from God, who descended into a certain virgin, and, being fashioned into flesh in her womb (*caro figuratus*) was born.

That is how Tertullian concludes his exposition.

Kaj Baago has pointed out[6] that for the first four centuries Christian theologians were open to a constructive dialogue with other faiths, and showed a real willingness to receive from them. The dialogue was perhaps not always in the politest terms, as a reading of Tertullian's *Apology* makes abundantly clear, yet the readiness to allow a constructive interaction with non Christian philosophy was certainly there. After the Constantinian settlement a hardening of attitude set in, which continued unabated until very recently. In Tertullian's exposition which we have just examined we see a fascinating example of this kind of 'growing' theology; and let us remember that it is given in his *Apology*, a piece of definite missionary writing. He speaks to Romans, to Stoics, to Philonic Jews. The message has been incorporated in our own western Theology and hymnology, and though it may not now speak to us in very convincing terms we should remember that in recent years those entrusted with the proclamation of the Gospel to both Muslims and Hindus have found it helpful – even if they were totally unaware that it originated with Tertullian and the Apologists!

### The word 'Person'

Another theological innovation of Tertullian was his use of the Latin word *persona*. We do not, of course, know for certain if Tertullian was in fact the first to use *persona* in this way – or for that matter *Trinitas* either. C. C. J. Webb points out that in Tertullian's time Latin had already become the language of ordinary theological discussion in the West; he was merely the

---

[6] In H. Jai Singh (ed.), *Inter-Religious Dialogue*, p. 127.

first to give it literary form.[7] Hippolytus, for example, who was a contemporary of Tertullian, and was himself a Roman, chose to write in Greek, as that was the literary convention. Many people may have been using these terms in their theological conversations, but Tertullian was the first to get it down in writing – and so he gets the credit!

In *Adv. Praxean* 12, Tertullian uses the word *persona* in commenting on God's words in Gen. 1. 26, 'Let *us* make man.' Why the plural? Tertullian replies:

Because the Son, the second person (*secunda persona*), God's own Word, was identified with him (*illi adhaerebat*); and also the third, the Spirit who is in the word. That is why he spoke in the plural.

This makes it clear, says Tertullian, that the Scripture makes a distinction between the persons.

He writes again:

I have come to the conclusion that you ought to accept the fact that there is (in God) *another* (subsistence); but it should be called *person* rather than substance, in order to denote distinction, not division.

What meaning does Tertullian give to the word *persona*? The Latin word originally means a player's mask, and hence came to be used of the characters of a drama – *dramatis personae*. Probably Tertullian uses it – following the custom of 'spoken' theology – as a translation of the Greek *prosopon*, which originally meant 'face' (not 'mask', which was *prosopeion*) and had therefore come to mean 'role' or 'aspect'. *Prosopon* in turn was sometimes used in Greek theology as a synonym of *hupostasis* which, as G. L. Prestige points out, normally meant the concrete objectivity or reality of a thing.[8] This would seem to indicate that when Tertullian says that the Son is a separate 'person' he really means that the Son 'plays a separate role' from the Father; like the ray in relation to the light, he does a different work, and is distinct in name and number, and yet essentially one with the Father.

[7] C. C. J. Webb, *God and Personality* (1918), p. 45.
[8] G. L. Prestige, *God in Patristic Thought* (1952), pp. xxviii, 168f., 188f.

The later idea of *persona* as meaning a separate centre of rationality came in much later with Boethius, who in the sixth century described it as 'the individual substance of a rational nature' (*persona est naturae rationabilis individua substantia*).[9] And *modern* ideas of 'personality' are a very much later creation, having their roots in the Romantic movement, in Kierkegaard and the existentialists, and in the writing of men like Webb, and above all Martin Buber. Today these ideas are always in our mind when we use the word 'person', and there is no harm in that; we should not be afraid of the new light which we receive from any quarter! But we need to remember that when Tertullian first described Christ as the second person he had in mind something much more like the 'independent, unchangeable subsistence'[10] implied by *hupostasis* and *prosopon* than the idea of a warm, individual character such as we imagine when we use the word 'person'. And yet, as Webb points out, Tertullian's *persona* does represent a step forward, for whereas *hupostasis* is a purely neutral word, *persona* can be applied only to rational creatures. So here, once more, we see a new interpretation of the inner relations of the Trinity, and the beginnings of a conception – that of *person* – which was to develop greatly in western theology.

## Augustine (354–430)

We shall deal with Augustine more briefly than Tertullian, not because he is less important, but because Tertullian was the pioneer of Latin theology, and our special interest is the tracing of the origins of terms and conceptions in a language not previously used for this purpose. We must, however, look for a moment at an important idea which Augustine brought into Latin theology.

It was Augustine who defined the inner relations of the Trinity in terms of doing rather than being, that is, in terms of relation rather than of essence or substance. The New Testament does indeed use the language of action rather than

[9] Quoted in Webb, *ibid.* p. 47.     [10] *Ibid.* p. 54.

essence; it refers to the Spirit as 'proceeding' from the Father (e.g. John 15. 26), and to the Father as having 'begotten' the Son (e.g. in Acts 13. 33, where Paul quotes Psalm 2. 7 'this day have I begotten thee – the Vulgate giving 'ego hodie *genui* te'). Augustine takes up these relationships of 'generation' and 'procession' and demonstrates in a variety of ways, and with a wealth of 'models', that the Trinity is not three separate substances, but is rather a Trinity of mutual interrelations. We may think, for example, of his fine description of the Spirit as the mutual love of Father and Son – the Lover, the Loved, and the Love which binds them together.

Augustine, as we have seen, was deeply influenced by Plato, and the Platonic threefold division of the human soul gives him a key or model which he uses often: the idea that in man there are united in one consciousness the three aspects of intellect, will and emotion. The particular form of the argument to which I now wish to turn is somewhat different, and comes in *De Civitate Dei* xi. 26, where he writes:

et *sumus* et nos esse *novimus*, et id esse et nosse *diligimus*:

'We *exist*; we *know* we exist; and we *rejoice* because of that knowledge and existence.'

That gives Augustine his 'model' for the inner relations of the Trinity. God exists; the Son is his Logos, his *ratio*, his knowledge; and the Spirit is the joy and love which unites the Father and Son in their mutual interrelatedness. We have seen something very like that before – in the *Sat, Cit, Ananda* which Keshub Chunder Sen used to describe the Trinity.

When a piece of what we might call 'Hindu natural theology' and an insight of one of the greatest Latin theologians correspond like that is it mere coincidence? Or is God perhaps through them both telling us something about what in fact the inner relations of the Trinity are?

In chapter 7 we are going to follow up this idea of the

underlying truth behind theological formulations. But first, in the chapter which follows, we shall continue to discuss the development of Latin theology, and shall give some thought to how Latin terminology has come to occupy such a dominant position in the English-speaking world.

# 5

## THE LATIN CAPTIVITY
## OF THE CHURCH

Latin was the language of the whole Western Church for 1,500 years, and has been the language of the Roman Catholic Church for another 400, although today its unique position even there has been very largely undermined. We would be foolish to imagine that those centuries have not left their mark. As a matter of fact, the theological and ecclesiastical vocabulary of the English language is saturated with Latin, as a visit even to any Protestant church on any Sunday morning will show.

We arrive at a Presbyterian church, for example, and take our seats in the *nave*, as the *transepts* are already filled by other members of the *congregation*. The *minister*, who happens also to be *Moderator* of the *General Assembly*, is still in the *vestry*. (The minister, by the way, is Latin, but the elders – perhaps significantly – are not!). We are glad to see the motto *Ardens sed virens* in one of the stained-glass windows, and on the chair behind the table we notice – with a sigh of satisfaction – the inscription *Primus inter Pares*. The *choir* comes in, and sings an *Introit*, and perhaps we rather regret the good old instrumentless days of the *precentor*. The minister leads us in prayers of *adoration, confession, supplication, petition* and *intercession*, and we may even heave a sigh of relief that we aren't Anglicans, with all those *collects* and *canticles* – *Te Deum, Magnificat, Nunc Dimittis* and all the rest. We do, however, have the *Creed*. The minister gives the *intimations*, including a notice about an *election* to the *Session*. Then the *offering* (or *collection*) is taken up, and we hear a good *sermon* on a well-chosen *text*. The minister is a good *expository* preacher. The service finally closes with the *benediction*.

Perhaps I have gone out of my way to select the italicised Latin words. But could you write a comparable paragraph using words other than Latin – say Greek, or Anglo-Saxon? Oddly enough, if you were to put the passage into German you would find that most of the Latin words disappeared, for German theology has a much less Latinised vocabulary than English. But there is no doubt that the 'style' of our Christian life in the English-speaking world is very deeply influenced by those thousand years of Latin dominance.

One of Luther's best known anti-Roman polemics is entitled *The Babylonish Captivity of the Church*. And even before the Reformation men like Wyclif, Hus and Erasmus had attacked the Roman Church for its Latinity and its Italian ness – among many other things! By the time the Reformation was an accomplished fact the Reformers had done much to loosen the Latin grip: they had broken the hold of the Vulgate, and had provided the Bible 'in the vulgar tongue', on the basis of the Hebrew and Greek texts; they had discarded the Latin liturgy, and provided liturgies or directories for public worship in the national languages; they had drawn up their own confessions, and broken away from the Roman teaching *magisterium*; they had severed their connection with the Roman ecclesiastical authority; they had set up their own systems of Church government, some of them radically different from the Roman pattern, others less so, but all intended to be 'conformable to the Word of God'.

This was a remarkable achievement, and the reformers were determined that the new Protestant Churches should be free from the tyranny of an unknown language and of a foreign *magisterium*. And yet there was much Latinity which they left untouched, or which was simply transliterated into English or French (using, of course, vernacular words already in use, but etymologically identical with the Latin ones). And it was not merely a question of language. It was also a matter of the ministry, of liturgy, of constitutions, of canon law, of the structure of Church courts, of administration, and simply of patterns of thought and logic. Let us look at some of these features in a little more detail.

### The influence of the Vulgate

We must never underestimate the importance of the Vulgate. It is a great book, with a great history. Yet it is a warning to us to beware of ever venerating *any* version of the Bible, for there comes a time when the best of versions outlives its usefulness. Jerome, working at the beginning of the fifth century, built on the foundation laid by various 'Old Latin' translations of the first four centuries (some of the first of them probably from North Africa). Today we can easily point out many in-adequacies in his version, but it has had an immense influence, not only on the Roman Catholic Church and official Latin terminology, but on the theological terminology of other languages, notably English. Jerome, Tertullian and Augustine between them account for a very high proportion of our basic biblical, theological and ecclesiastical vocabulary.

There are many echoes of the Vulgate even in the Authorised Version, especially, perhaps, in some of the more theological passages of Paul, where a technical vocabulary is used. Take, for example, Rom. 3. 24–5:

Justificati gratis per gratiam ipsius, per redemptionem, quae est in Christo Jesu, quem proposuit Deus propitiationem per fidem in sanguine ipsius, ad ostensionem justitiae suae, propter remissionem praecedentium delictorum.

'Being justified freely by his grace through the redemption that is in Christ Jesus: whom God hath set forth to be a propitiation through faith in his blood, to declare his righteousness for the remission of sins that are past.'

We remember, of course, that the translators of the AV worked straight from the Greek; they had, however, echoes of the Vulgate, and of earlier English translations made from the

Vulgate – like that of Coverdale – sounding in their ears, and this no doubt influenced their choice of words. Three things here are worth noticing: first, the words justified, grace, redemption, propitiation, remission, are taken straight from the Latin; secondly, the translators were aware that 'justice' (from *justitia*) would be a misleading translation of the Greek *dikaiosune*, and so chose the more positive and less legalistic 'righteousness'; thirdly, the Greek word *hilasterion* puzzled them – as well it might! They decided to accept the Latin word *propitiatio* in its English form and as a result have confused many good Christians ever since and sent many a preacher hurrying to his commentaries.

That example gives us a fair idea of how Vulgate-influenced some parts – and some very important parts – of the Authorised Version are. One still occasionally hears protests – not least, oddly enough, in India – when a new translation proves to use a word different from the Authorised Version. Usually the protesters are unaware that they are in fact asking to retain the vocabulary of the Vulgate, which Luther renounced so long ago.

(One might note in passing that even new translations do not always avoid Latinisms. In this passage the New English Bible retains 'justified' and – surprisingly – 'justice'; substitutes 'liberation' for the AV 'redemption' (Greek *apolutrosis*) and paraphrases *hilasterion* as 'the means of expiating sin'.)

As another example of a Latin word which found its way into the AV and changed the meaning of the Greek original we could take the familiar 'charity' of 1 Cor. 13, taken from the Vulgate *caritas* for *agape*. The fault here was not indeed Jerome's, but rather that of the English language, which downgraded the word 'charity' after 1611. I think it was James Moffatt who managed to persuade people that '*love*' was a better translation, and most recent translations have followed him.

On the whole the tendency of the Vulgate, as against the Greek, was to stress the legalistic aspect of the terms used, and perhaps even to introduce a legalistic overtone where none was intended. Of course there is a forensic element in Paul's use of terms like *dikaioun*,[1] *dikaiosune*, etc. Yet in the Vulgate the forensic bias is strengthened, and perhaps something of the grace and liberty is lost. We have already looked at *paenitentia* for *metanoia*, and *justitia* for *dikaiosune*. Think also of *justificare* 'to *make* just' for *dikaioun*, and *sanctificare* 'to make holy' for *hagiazein*. The word *electio* seems to be more legalistic than *klesis*. And *vita aeterna* substitutes endless quantity for the new quality of *zoe aionios*. These are just a few random examples, yet they make one realise why an Indian theologian like P. Chenchiah could write, 'The juridical conception of Christianity is an attempt to reduce Jesus to the ideology of Judaism or the political ideology of the State of Rome: in other words to interpret Jesus in terms of sacrifice and propitiation in law, offence and punishment.'[2]

### Extra-biblical Latin terminology

To give a detailed exposition of Latin theological terminology would be an enterprise far beyond the scope of this book. Some of the extra-biblical Latin terms do, however, further illustrate the point that the Greek meaning can be subtly changed, and often in a legalistic direction. Take the interesting word *sacramentum*, for example, a word which is not strictly extra-biblical as it is found in the Vulgate (e.g. in Eph. 5. 32 and Rev. 1. 20) as a translation of the Greek word *musterion* – not, however, in the modern sense of 'sacrament'. Originally the word had a juridical connotation in civil or military affairs, such as the oath of allegiance administered by a commander in the enlistment of troops; but it acquired the general sense of a solemn *sign* – an outward action or pledge signifying something sacred and inward. The word used by the Greek Church for the sacraments – *musterion*, or the 'holy mysteries' – is much more neutral in meaning. In a sense, then, the whole nexus of ideas called 'sacramental theology' is a deduction

---

[1] For a discussion of this point see *Report of Gen. Assembly of Presb. Church in Ireland* (1971), p. 9.

[2] Chenchiah, *Rethinking Christianity in India*, p. 164.

from a Latin word, which would not have followed so readily from the Greek.

It is interesting to note that it is not simply the Roman Catholic Church which uses Latin terminology, though one can of course point immediately to many words with a 'Catholic' aura: merit, indulgence, purgatory, assumption, host, transubstantiation – the list could be endless. But evangelical Christians draw most of their vocabulary from the same milieu: decree, predestination, election, conversion, substitution, satisfaction, vicarious, plenary, imputation, original (sin), etc. Both Protestant and Roman Catholic theologians and preachers draw on the same rich source of Latin terminology, a terminology which had already reached approximately its present extent before the Reformation.

### The Reformers and the Latin tradition

Luther and Calvin had learnt their theology in Latin, and Calvin at least – because of the structure of the French language – had no choice but to use Latin terminology and also a Latin way of looking at things. He was an enthusiastic Latinist[3] and we must remember that the Reformers, as children of the Renaissance and contemporaries of Erasmus, were under the spell of the rediscovered Greek and Latin classics; they were breaking away from the chains of medieval ecclesiastical Latin, and one of their instruments of escape was the Latin of Cicero.[4] In his youth Calvin wrote a book on Seneca, and he delighted in publishing the Institutes in Latin. One of his main concerns was, indeed, to escape from the Latin captivity of the Church, yet there were many Latin inheritances which he omitted to repudiate.

I spent a semester in Basel in 1953–4, and vividly remember Karl Barth speaking of this in a seminar on Calvin. He pointed out how Calvin had unquestioningly accepted the natural theology of Aquinas, and inserted it in the Institutes; and how

---

[3] Cf. G. D. Henderson, *Presbyterianism* (Aberdeen, 1954), p. 20.
[4] *Ibid.* p. 23.

in his teaching on predestination and election he had per-
petuated the old error of dealing with the subject as though
Christ did not exist (*remoto Christo*), and so had landed himself
in the appalling difficulty of double predestination. Barth, of
course, set himself to the task of rectifying Calvin's lapses!

Calvin, the great systematiser of the Reformation, rejected
Aquinas in many things – for example in the doctrine of
transubstantiation. He did not, however, reject the Aristotelian
type of logic, and indeed the Institutes is a very good example
of that logical method which endeared itself so much to the
Reformers and their seventeenth-century successors. Calvin's
legal training, and his logical mind as well as the Latinity of
his vocabulary, are very clear on every page. He adhered to
Aquinas also in the structure of the Institutes; in fact the
traditional order of the treatment of the doctrines – the threefold division based on the Trinity – goes right back to the early
*Regula Fidei* and to the Apostles' and Nicene Creeds. Calvin
did not feel any call to depart from the traditional order.

### Protestant scholasticism

By the middle of the seventeenth century the enthusiasm and
freedom of the Reformation had largely evaporated and theology had become harder, more formal and more rationalistic.
To quote Lecerf, 'Reformed theology became Cartesian in the
17th century, and thus formally rationalistic, while remaining
all the time materially orthodox.'[5] Even the Westminster Confession cannot escape the charge of scholasticism and formalism,
in comparison, say, with the fresher Scots Confession of 1560,
which, however, lacked that detailed comprehensiveness desired
by the Westminster divines in 1643 and warmly welcomed
by the Scottish General Assembly of 1647. Here is how a modern
exponent of the Westminster Confession, G. S. Hendry, describes it:

The manner of approach is excessively legalistic. This was characteristic of the period, which was preoccupied by constitutional

[5] A. Lecerf, *An Introduction to Reformed Dogmatics* (1949), p. 22.

questions. . . . The Confession has more of the character of a constitutional than a confessional document. This is reflected in the
style; with its precise phrasing, it cumbrous involutions and repeti-
tions, the multiplication of prepositions and qualifying clauses, it
often sounds like a legal contract. . . . It is a question whether this
kind of language (and the mentality that goes with it) is the best
medium for the presentation of the doctrine of the gospel.[6]

As a brief test of this alleged legalism, let us once more
examine a short section of the Confession (xi. i, *Of Justification*,
slightly abridged; words of Latin origin have been italicised):

Those whom God *effectually* calleth, he also freely *justifieth*: not by
*infusing* righteousness into them, but by pardoning their sins, and by
*accounting* and *accepting* their *persons* as righteous . . . not by *imputing*
faith itself, the act of believing, or any other evangelical *obedience*
to them, as their righteousness; but by *imputing* the *obedience* and
*satisfaction* of Christ unto them

The phrase 'not by infusing righteousness' is a direct rejection
of Roman Catholic doctrine, so we cannot complain about its
Latin origins. The legalistic note, however – the note of
juridical transaction – is rather strongly present in the words
'accounting', 'imputing' and 'satisfaction'. The point which is
being made is, of course, a valid and indeed a vital one; no
works of ours – not even our faith – can be counted as righteousness which would put us right with God; it is only when we
trust Christ completely that *his* righteousness comes to our aid;
we are accepted as righteous by God for *his* sake. As Hendry
says, 'The evangelical doctrine of justification expresses the
heart of the gospel – that he who accepts Christ is accepted.'
It is true that a legalistic Roman doctrine is being rejected
here; true also that Paul himself uses legalistic terminology.
Yet one cannot help feeling that the whole paragraph gives –
and perhaps especially in a country with a spiritual tradition
like India – a wrong impression that the Gospel is inseparably
bound up with legalism.

Leaving the Westminster Confession now, we may note that
later manuals of conservative reformed dogmatics, like those of

[6] Hendry, *op cit.* pp. 14, 15.

Heppe, Charles Hodge and A. A. Hodge, Louis Berkhof and others, tend to preserve the same tradition of Latinity, logic and legalism. This is not to say that they are not both useful and important. They are; and I doubt if any reformed student of theology has a right to talk about systematic theology until he has grappled with some of these great men, and has understood, appreciated, and seen both the strength and the beauty of the underlying structure. Barth used to send his students back to Wollebius (in Latin!) and Heppe, and it was an excellent discipline!

### Church structures

We have said enough about the Latin language, and Latin ways of thought and legalistic tendencies. Now we must turn to consider some of the Church-structures which we have inherited. And for a moment, before we go on to talk about the organisation of the Church let us glance at some of the actual structures in stone and brick which we see around us. The Romans passed on to the Church the basilica type of building, which was originally a design for public meeting-halls in the Roman Empire. The general shape, with a long colonnaded nave and circular apse, survived through various styles, notably Romanesque, Norman and Gothic. And it is still with us. Seventeenth- and eighteenth-century Presbyterian 'meeting houses' in Ireland, and dissenting chapels in England and Wales broke away from that tradition in their four-square solidity, but from about 1865 the fashion for Gothic captured even these citadels, and thousands of Protestants are still to-day under this particular form of Latin captivity from which, judging by many excellent buildings, Rome itself has broken free![7]

Much of the ecclesiastical structure of the Roman Church survived in the Lutheran and Anglican Churches, where the break with the past was less radical than in the Calvinistic

[7] Cf. A. L. Drummond, *The Church Architecture of Protestantism* (1934), pp. 4ff.

tradition. Lutherans and Anglicans retained a liturgy which, though now in the vernacular, was really a suitably amended version of the Roman rite. The threefold ministry of bishop, priest and deacon was also retained, and in some cases, e.g., England and Sweden, care was taken to maintain the apostolic succession. The diocesan structure also survived.

Calvin's desire was to 'restore the ancient face of the Catholic Church', and in order to achieve this end he was much more radical and iconoclastic than Luther or the Anglican Reformers. The whole Roman structure, including the threefold ministry, the diocesan organisation and the liturgy, was swept away, and in its place an effort was made to return to an idealised and adapted form of the organisation of the early Church. But the legalistic, logical and organising habit was far too strong in Calvin and Knox for them to be able to return to an atmosphere at all like that of the early Church. The pre-Reformation structure was totally changed, and soon a highly organised new structure emerged, democratic to an extent, no doubt, but still highly sophisticated, and set around by many legal safeguards. The Presbyterian system of Church government may indeed – as it affirms – be 'founded on and agreeable to the Word of God', but it bears the marks of Roman law and legalistic institutionalism to no small degree. This can be seen even in the early *Books of Discipline*, or in the *Form of Presbyterian Church Government* of 1645 – to say nothing of current constitutions and codes.

When Church organisation of this kind is transplanted to a country like India it appears very foreign, very legalistic, and very unspiritual. In the words of a French monk who has lived many years in India, 'To Hindu eyes Christian churches appear to be wonderfully organised bodies. Their administration is remarkable, their worship is conducted with an order and discipline which many Hindus would like to see emulated in their own temples. Christian theology bears the mark of reason and logic.' Yet to the Hindu, he adds, these 'externals of religion' have 'nothing to do in the last resort with real spiritual life, with *moksa* or salvation'.[8] This is true.

---

[8] Swami Abhishiktananda, *The Church in India*, p. 14.

But besides discouraging the interested Hindu, this type of Church structure – whether Presbyterian, Anglican or Roman Catholic in its origins – has very questionable effects on Christians as well. India is a legalistically minded country, and 'going to court' a popular pursuit; and this type of Church organisation provides unlimited scope for litigiousness. It is not uncommon for a church-member to be more devoted to his Church *constitution* than to his Bible, and this is clearly very dangerous for the life of the Church. What happens is that the structure, the machine, becomes more important, more demanding, more time-consuming than the work of witness and service. Whether the structure is authoritarian or demo-cratic, if it interferes with the life of the Body it should be drastically modified or even abandoned. For the Church is the Body of Christ. He is the Lord of the Church; he is the norm; and if the Body is hindered from being active and loving and self-sacrificing, then all our organisation is useless. Criticism like this is of course nothing new. Men like Hans Küng and Charles Davis are making it in Europe and America. In India writers like Manilal Parekh and P. Chenchiah made it fifty years ago, and Kaj Baago, Subba Rao and others have made it again in recent days. It is sometimes convenient to forget, and it is invariably hard to practise the motto of the Reforma-tion – a Latin one at that! – *ecclesia semper reformanda.*

### The legacy of Caesaropapism

In the time of the early Church, Christians were frequently per-secuted by the State, and the Church had to resist the claims of the pagan Emperor which conflicted with its loyalty to Christ. With the conversion of Constantine everything changed, and there began that uneasy alliance between Church and State which in various forms has continued to haunt the Church ever since. In the eastern Empire the Emperor exercised con-trol over the Church; in the West there was greater free-dom for the Church until the establishment of the Holy

Roman Empire and the claims of the Carolingian and German emperors. In medieval Christendom there was a precarious balance of actual power, though in theory Church and State were united in a single culture.[9] It was this unity of Church and State which made possible the Crusades, and later the Portuguese *Padroado*, two enterprises which have never been forgotten in non-Christian lands, and which have given rise to an almost automatic antipathy to Christian evangelism on the side of Muslims and Hindus.

The Reformation did not end the close connection between Church and State, but simply altered it. Luther soon found himself in alliance with those German princes who accepted the Reformation, and in opposition to those who continued, for various reasons, to support the papacy. In the words of Charles Davis, 'in each of the confessional regions the politico-ecclesiastical unity of Christendom was maintained as the norm'[10] and this frequently resulted in a privileged position for those who shared the faith of the ruler, and the denial of religious freedom for those who did not. *Cuius regio eius religio* – to use yet another of those very useful Latin tags!

One of the most thoroughgoing experiments in the interlocking of Church and State was that of Calvin at Geneva, followed by Knox in Scotland. The English Reformation and Settlement, and the theory of the divine right of kings was yet another demonstration of the same principle. So was the Commonwealth, and the Restoration. In fact throughout Europe the theory was virtually unchallenged until the eighteenth-century Enlightenment and the French Revolution, though many Christians in many lands gave up the struggle and sought for freedom from politico-ecclesiastical control in lands beyond the sea.

Today in large areas of the world the link between Church and State is severed, or is fairly nominal, as in England and Scotland. There are, however, a few pockets where it remains, though sometimes in a crypto rather than an open form. And

[9] Cf. Charles Davis, *God's Grace in History* (1966), pp. 26, 27.
[10] *Ibid.* p. 27.

theocratic states are not limited to the residuary legatees of Christendom, for many of the Muslim states come into this category.

The idea itself is of course found in the Old Testament, but the form in which it has come down to us is really a Latin one, and goes back in a continuous line to the 'official' religion of pre-Christian imperial Rome and the persecuting Emperors of the early Church. The Empire became Christian, but the urge to enforce conformity continued, though now in an inverted way, for it was the Christians who ruled and the pagans who had to conform. For a time, perhaps, for example in the religiously monochrome Europe of the thirteenth century, it was a noble ideal, the vision of a human society entirely subservient to Christian principles. But in a pluralistic society it could not fail to lead to oppression, whether in a society where Protestant lived beside Roman Catholic or one where Christian rubbed shoulders with non-Christian.

The French Revolution established secularism, and gradually this ideal has come to be accepted in many countries. We have already noticed how India after its independence in 1947 became a secular state, and how this policy is of great importance for the freedom and prosperity of the 14 million Christians in that predominantly Hindu country. To quote Charles Davis once more, 'The function in religious matters of the State is to establish and guarantee conditions of religious freedom for all its citizens, whatever their belief, within the limits of public order.'[11] The Roman Catholic Church itself has accepted the principle in the Declaration on Religious Freedom of Vatican II. We shall be returning to this question of the secular state in a later chapter. Meantime let us simply remember that the view that the Church or a religiously committed power-group should exercise control over the State is one of our Latin legacies, which we constantly need to re-examine, not merely in the light of our 'subordinate standards', but above all in the light of our primary standard; and not simply in the light of Romans 13, but also in the light of Acts 4. 19–20, which in

[11] *Ibid.* p. 29.

the Authorised Version reads, 'Whether it be right in the sight of God to hearken unto you more than unto God, judge ye. For we cannot but speak the things which we have seen and heard'.

I may have appeared over-critical of the Latin strain in the life of the western Church. Our debt to the Latin language, to Roman civilisation, and to Latin ways of thought is immense. Personally I love the Latin language, and find myself deeply moved by some of the great Latin hymns of the Church, like *Angularis fundamentum* (Christ is made the sure foundation), or *O quanta qualia* (O what their joy and their glory). Anyone who has ever taken part in a choir singing Bach's B-Minor Mass will know what I mean. Magnificent – Yes! But is it not time that we asked ourselves how much longer we are going to yield uncritical allegiance to this tradition which still so strangely dominates us? I have some friends among young Indian Roman Catholic seminarians in Ahmedabad. They do not today study Latin in their training for the priesthood; not *at all*. They *do* study Greek and Hebrew and Indian languages, as well as English. The new Gujarati liturgy they use is less influenced by Latinity than are many of the prayers one hears in Presbyterian or Methodist Churches. The Roman Catholic Church has advanced quite a long way along the road *away* from Latinity.

What about the rest of us?

# 6

# THE UNIVERSAL SIGNIFICANCE OF
# INDIAN CHRISTIAN THEOLOGY

In our last chapter we saw how Latin patterns of vocabulary and thought, as well as Roman methods of organisation and a Roman tendency to link Church and State have impressed themselves on the Christianity of the West. And it is not merely that Christian life and thought in western countries are deeply coloured by this pattern; even the Church in India has, through its many western contacts, been strongly stained in the same way. Now, however, the Indian Church has realised its cultural identity with the Indian tradition, and, as we have seen, a distinctive Indian Christian theology has appeared, firmly based on the Christian Scriptures, and yet responsive to the thought-forms of Indian philosophy and culture. A great many people today would agree – fifty years ago they might have been more dubious – that such a culturally integrated theology is necessary for the task of proclamation and witness in India. But is it possible for us to go any further? Could this emerging Indian theology have something significant to say to the West – to us? The gentiles *did* come to the light of Christ; they brought their gold and incense (Isaiah 60. 3 and 6). We of the West were gentiles, and we have tried to bring our gifts, but now others are coming too, and they come from a rich and generous land – rich, that is, in the things of the spirit. A modern British theologian, Ninian Smart, has written, 'The Christian experience as hitherto understood can be enriched by the insights of the multitudinous traditions of India.'[1] And Chenchiah of Madras – perhaps at the time an

[1] Ninian Smart, *The Yogi and the Devotee* (1968), p. 168.

73

amateur dabbler in photography – has given us a vivid illustration: 'The negative plate of Jesus developed in a solution of Hinduism brings out hitherto unknown features of the portrait and these may prove exactly the "Gospel" for our time.'[2]

### *New Light* for *India*

It is important that we should see the relations between the Indian Church and the Church in western countries as a two-way traffic. There was a time when the relation of the Indian Church to the 'missionary' Churches was one of dependence. Then came the urge for independence. Today, however, we can look each other in the eye as fellow-partners in the Church of Christ, in a relation of interdependence – 'every one members one of another'. When Sadhu Sundar Singh visited Europe, America and Australia in 1920 and 1922 he was able to draw far greater crowds than a western evangelist would usually do in India. And in recent years the Indian Churches have sent their own missionaries to many countries, including East Africa, Fiji, Nepal and Japan. And in the realm of thought too, it is important that we should learn from one another. So first of all, let us look at some of the new features which Christian thought has brought to India, giving a new insight at points where on the whole Indian philosophy had been less than positive.

*The person.* First of all there is the question of the value of the individual person. Hinduism tended to look simply at the soul, the *ātman*, which remains unchanged through successive incarnations; but there was little concern for the individual person, in all his surroundings and his difficulties. The idea that God cares for each one of us individually, and that we must care for each other in love and concern, is not strong in Hinduism. The idea of duty is there, and also a somewhat detached 'compassion', but the warm, human, disinterested

[2] *Rethinking Christianity in India* (Madras, 1938), p. 162.

conception of *agape* is something which is missing in Hinduism, though Gandhi's interpretation of *ahiṃsā* or non-violence sometimes comes very near it.

*Creation.* Secondly, Hinduism takes a rather negative view of the created world, usually viewing it as *māyā*, or illusion – something less than real. Christianity looks on creation as the work of God's love, and on created things as good – to be used, not abused. Thus while for many Hindus the way to salvation is the way of asceticism, of suppression of the body, Christians believe that we have a responsibility to use all God's created gifts, including the human body, to his glory.

*Purpose in history.* Thirdly, there is the question of history. The Hindu view was that history is cyclic; one age succeeds another until the wheel turns full circle and we are back where we started. That was the Greek idea also. But the Jewish tradition, which Christianity has inherited, is different: God's purpose is at work all the time – in creation, in the choice of Abraham, in the history of Israel, in the coming and the death of Christ, in the growth of the Church, in the events of the secular world. And everything is moving forwards towards a goal; God's purpose is at work in history. This is something which gives a purpose to our life, and helps us to plan our projects, and carry them out.

One may notice, perhaps, that these three points are all things which many 'secular humanists' might share with Christians; they have almost become part of western man's way of looking at things, part of the outlook of the secular society. Yet there is no doubt that they come from the Judaeo-Christian tradition, and not from any other. Recent Indian Christian writers like P. D. Devanandan and M. M. Thomas have pointed out how these ideas are a real and vital contribution of Christianity to modern India; they are ideas which have helped India to become a progressive, secular state, and have helped to 'humanise' society; to draw man's attention to the fact that all men are entitled to enough to eat, to a house to live in, to employment, to freedom, and that we are all committed to improving the lot of our fellow human-beings. Swami Vivekananda and Mahatma Gandhi did much to make these ideals part of Indian life; but they were *new* ideas for Hinduism, and owe much to the new influx of light and service which the Christian Church – with all its defects – brought to India.

Here is how a great lover of India, the French Abbé Jules Monchanin, described the kind of two-way traffic in ideas which we are considering:

> India must give the West a keener sense of the eternal, of the primacy of Being over Becoming, and receive, in turn, from the West a more concrete sense of the temporal, of becoming, of the person, of love (of which India, alas! knows so little).[3]

## *New Light* from *India*

Now we must look at some of the special insights which have emerged in Indian theology, and which can be of help to us in the West.

### *The Pramāṇas – our sources of authority*
We know how keen the Reformers were on determining their sources of authority, over against the *magisterium* of the Roman Church. The primary standard was the Word of God, the Scriptures of the Old and New Testaments, interpreted by the Holy Spirit, in the light of Scripture itself, as the Christian studies his Bible, by comparing passage with passage. The subordinate standards were the Confessions, which the Reformers and their successors drew up, and which were regarded as biblical teaching in a nutshell. What is the position in Indian theology?

A. J. Appasamy[4] has pointed out that Hinduism traditionally has three 'standards' or *pramāṇas* – scripture (*śruti*), experience (*anubhava*) and inference (*anumāna*). This is an interesting trio.

---

[3] *Swami Parama Arubi Anandam* (Tiruchirapalli, 1959), p. 222.

[4] A. J. Appasamy, *What Shall We Believe? A Study in Christian Pramanas* (Madras, 1971).

*Śruti.* This word (from the root *śru*) means 'hearing', and was applied to the Vedas, which the prophets or *rishis* were said to have 'heard' directly from God. The word also has a derived meaning of 'revelation' – God's will revealed to man in Scripture. How does the word compare in usefulness with our 'revelation'?

*Revelatio* is another Latin word, from *re-velare* which means to unveil, and it is used as a translation of the NT Greek word *apokalupsis*, which has the same meaning. In other words, our word for 'revelation' is related to the sense of sight. Now the Bible undoubtedly has many examples of people, like Isaiah or Paul, whose conversion or call took place through a vision. India has many similar examples, like Sundar Singh or Paul Sudhakar. Yet the usual way in which men come to God in Christ is through the *Word*, and through hearing (*ex auditu*). After all, hearing is a better medium for communication than sight; sound radio conveys a message, but TV without the sound is meaningless. When Marshal McLuhan wrote *The Gutenberg Galaxy* he was questioning the value of the *printed* word in a multi-media age; he was not challenging the value of the *word* itself, which can be spoken or written. Pictures, symbols, gestures can make the word more vivid, more easy to appropriate, but they cannot replace it.

When we read or hear the *Śruti*, Jesus the living word, *Śabda*, confronts us through the read or spoken word; and through that *hearing* he comes to us. And that we call *Śruti* – the *heard* communication of revelation. It seems to me that this term – linking hearing and revelation, and linking them both to the *Word*, is a better term than revelation. It can certainly deepen our understanding of what God is doing when we read the Bible.

*Anubhava.* The second *pramāṇa* is experience. A story is told of the young Swami Vivekananda. He was going through a period of searching for truth and went from *guru* to *guru*, seeking for the *sadguru* (the real or true teacher), as is the way in India. To each he put the question 'Have you seen God?', but no one could give a straight answer until he came to Sri Ramakrishna, who answered 'Yes'. Vivekananda became his disciple, for he wanted someone who could lead him straight into the presence of God. The Indian seeker after God is not looking for intellectual knowledge, but for experience – for the immediate experience, eye-to-eye as it were, of *pratyakṣa anubhava*. For the followers of the *bhakti mārga* this may come in an emotional feeling of loving communion with God: for the *advaitin* it may be a more intellectual contemplation, when all the illusion of *māyā* is left behind, and the soul experiences its oneness with the world-soul, *Brahman*.

For Christians this is a matter of great importance. It puts an end to mere theological speculation. If we want to know anything *about* God, the only way is to *know* God. Direct, unmediated experience of God in Christ is what qualifies us to act as missionaries, as *gurus*. Here is how Swami Abhishikt-ananda describes the true *guru*: 'He is the man who knows through personal and intimate experience the truth of what he teaches and is able to lead his disciple not to formulas, rites or new ways of life, but straight up to the awareness of the divine Presence.'[5]

This is the kind of experience which Paul mentions in 2 Cor. 12. 2 – how he was 'in Christ', and caught up into the third heaven. It is the experience envisaged in the words 'Abide in me,' in John 15. 4. And without such an experience we know nothing of the Christian faith, and are not entitled to speak about it to others. The whole Indian approach to the life of the spirit makes this abundantly clear: that experience of God is essential, if we are to claim that we are Christians.

It is fashionable in the West to distrust experience, and no doubt it can be something shallow and emotional. But Indian theology makes it clear that there is no Christianity without it. This is not just a sort of reinstatement of Schleiermacher's view of religion as the feeling of utter dependence; it is a sober insistence on the fact that theology, and even Bible study, is not enough. There must be experience and commitment.

[5] *The Church in India*, p. 19.

*Anumāna.* The third *pramāṇa* is inference, and it need not detain us. Under it will come our 'subordinate standards', which are deduced by inference from Scripture, and must be in accordance with Scripture.

So there are the three standards. I believe they give us a clearer idea of the meaning of Scripture and revelation, and that the insistence on experience is something which we need to follow in our own practice. Jesus is the centre of our theology and our life. In Hans Küng's words, he must be decisive for us; and that means that we must hear his word; meet him in a real encounter, and accept him. Only then can we speak.

## *The meaning of faith*

The two greatest insights of Luther's Reformation were the return to Scripture and to justification by faith. Luther called the latter the article 'by which the Church stands or falls' (*stantis et cadentis ecclesiae*), and he was right. He was by-passing the whole edifice of good works and merit, and the machinery for their operation which had been set up by the medieval Church, and was returning to Paul's great insight expressed so clearly in Galatians and Romans.

But what do we mean by 'faith'? Even within the Protestant tradition the meaning of this great word has often been obscured. We speak of subscription to the Confession of Faith – and what do we mean? I am afraid that we usually mean 'assent to the teaching', or perhaps even 'submission to the authority'. We speak of 'the Christian faith', or 'other faiths', meaning a comprehensive religious system. Sometimes 'faith' can mean simply credulity – like the White Queen in *Through the Looking Glass* who sometimes succeeded in believing as many as six impossible things before breakfast. In the New Testament the word *pistis* is sometimes used for 'the Christian faith', especially in the Pastoral Epistles. But its normal meaning is neither assent, nor credulity, nor what Roman Catholic critics of Protestantism call 'fideism'; it means trust, self-commitment, total surrender to a person. It is that kind of faith that 'justifies' – that puts us right with God.

In the Sanskritic languages there are several words which are used for faith, the commonest being *viśvās*, and another – less used by Christians because of its Hindu overtones – *śraddhā*. These words are quite good, and they do express the idea of trust in a person. Yet there is another word which perhaps even more clearly expresses what Luther had in mind, and that is the word *bhakti* – a word which implies worship, and total surrender to God. We have already seen how the 'way of *bhakti*' is one of the three traditional 'ways' of Hinduism, and how A. J. Appasamy and others have given it a Christian exposition. Appasamy wrote a book called *Christianity as Bhakti Marga*,[6] which is really a study of the Johannine doctrine of Love, and he shows how *bhakti* means total self-surrender to God, with no attempt to justify oneself by one's own good works; only God's grace can save us – not our own faith. This is an important point, because we often fall into error by speaking of 'justification by faith', as if our faith were a work, a meritorious achievement of our own. What we mean – and what Paul meant – is justification *by God's grace*, in the context of our loving, total, obedient surrender to Him. The word *bhakti* can include all that.

Let me quote four lines from one of the great Hindu *bhakti* poets, Tukaram, and we shall see how close he comes to our ideal of surrender in faith:

> I am a mass of sin;
> Thou art all purity;
> Yet Thou must take me as I am
> And bear my load for me.[7]

Narayan Vaman Tilak, the Christian poet of *bhakti*, said that he had journeyed by the bridge of Tukaram to the feet of Christ. Here, in this very rich concept of *bhakti*, is a ray of light from India which can deepen our understanding of the simple-

---

[6] A. J. Appasamy, *Christianity as Bhakti Marga* (Madras, 1928).
[7] Quoted in A. J. Appasamy, *The Gospel and India's Heritage* (1942), p. 125. Translation by Nicol Macnicol.

hearted surrender and obedience which are implied in the word 'faith'.

### 'The fourfold ideal'

The word Indian Christians most commonly use for salvation is *mokṣa* or *mukti* (both from the same root). *Mukti* also means 'liberation'. Recently not a few Christians were startled to hear that the Bangladesh army of liberation called itself the 'Mukti Fauj', for to them that expression had only one meaning – Salvation Army! In our second chapter we mentioned briefly the fourfold description of *mokṣa* or *mukti* (liberation) which is traditional in the *bhakti* tradition, and which has been given a Christian interpretation by Paul Sudhakar and others. The four words are:

*Sālokya* or co-existence, in the same realm
*sāmīpya* or con-frontation, encounter
*sārupya* or con-formation
*sāyujya* or communion.

Sudhakar says that this fourfold relationship describes man as God meant him to be; Adam, made in God's image, had all of these, but through sin man has lost them. In Christ, however, the fourfold ideal can be restored.

Just to demonstrate the 'richness' of this conception, let me point out two contexts in which I myself have found it very helpful. The first is in describing – in preaching or 'dialogue' – what Presbyterians traditionally call 'the way of salvation'. At first the 'pilgrim' (for Bunyan and the *bhakti mārga* are on the same wavelength!) comes into the 'realm' (*loka*) of God's people; perhaps he goes to church, or to a meeting, or meets a Christian friend, or reads a Christian book. There he hears – or reads – the Word, and through the Word comes to an encounter, *sāmīpya*, with Christ, the Living Word. Here I would change the order of the four, placing next *sāyujya* or communion, 'faith-union'. The root *yuj* means a yoke (cognate with the Greek *zugos* and Latin *iugum*), and the word means 'being yoked together', like two oxen to the same cart. We are joined with

Christ, taking his yoke upon us, 'abiding' in him. And because of that we go on to the final stage, *sārupya*, when we become like Christ, not because of our merit or virtue or even our faith, but because of his grace (e.g., Rom. 12. 2; Phil. 2. 5–8).

The second context is that of prayer, as we seek to penetrate deeper and deeper into fellowship with God. We begin, as it were, in the outer court, with our reading of the Word, and meditation on it. That brings us on to encounter with Christ, and then to the experience (*anubhava*) of union or communion with him. There we rest for a time, and then return to the world, changed because of what has happened, and with his joy in our hearts, and his light in our faces.

## Saccidānanda

In 1963 Bishop Robinson published *Honest to God*. I do not propose to give an analysis of the book, but I do wish to say something about one part where Robinson seems to me to come very close to a Hindu (*advaita*) position, and also to involve himself in contradictions.[8] And I believe that we can perhaps go a long way towards solving his problem by the use of the Trinitarian concept of *Saccidānanda*, which we have already examined.

Briefly, Robinson tries to combine insights from Tillich and Bonhöffer. Following Tillich, he speaks of God as 'the ground of our Being'. 'Authentic existence' – his word, perhaps, for *mokṣa*! – comes when we 'integrate' with this ground of being. That is a very close approximation to the *advaita* doctrine of the union of the human spirit (*jivātman*) with the Supreme Spirit (*paramātman*), and I have it on good authority that although Tillich never visited India, his widow, who did pay a visit after his death, felt that the Indian view of life was one that would have greatly attracted her husband, had he had the opportunity of experiencing it.

That statement, however, leaves little or no room for Christ, and Robinson therefore selects a phrase from Bonhöffer (who was perhaps much more orthodox and even evangelical than some of his followers imagine) – the phrase 'the man for others'.

[8] J. A. T. Robinson, *Honest to God* (1963), chaps. 3 and 4.

For Robinson, then, Jesus is 'the man for others', who empties himself of self, and lives entirely for others, so demonstrating his true nature. The trouble with this picture – attractive as it is in a way – is that it breaks the link, the co-essentiality if you like, between Father and Son. God is the Absolute, Christ is the man for others, and there is no essential unity between them. In other words, the *homoousion*, which the early Church arrived at after such long controversy, and which we preserve in the Nicene Creed as well as the Westminster Confession, is dropped.

Now let us look at *Saccidānanda*. Is there a place here for the conception of 'ground of being'? Yes, there is. *Saccidānanda* is the description of *Brahman*, the highest point, according to Indian thought, to which 'natural theology' will take us. And *Brahman* undoubtedly *is* the ground of being, the *Paramātman* with whom the *jivātman* can find union. The trouble with Tillich is that he describes our relation with *Brahman* but forgets that *Brahman* is essentially triune; that *Cit* and *Ānanda* – the Logos and the joy of the Spirit – are the essential inner relations of the Trinity, and that it is through the Logos that the Absolute makes himself known.

Jesus said 'No man comes to the Father but by me' (John 14. 6). That sentence says two very important things, one a critique of much of Hinduism, and one a critique of much of Christianity. First, it says that if we want to come to God – to the Truth, Reality, *Sat* – the way is through Christ, the Logos who became incarnate in Jesus of Nazareth. If we want to know what God is like, we look at the face of Jesus. If we want union with God, the first step is to encounter Jesus and surrender to Him. That is what we need to say very clearly in our dialogue with Hindu, and other, friends. But secondly – and this too is very important – we are to *go on to the Father*. There are many Christians who have settled for something less than a full Trinitarian religion; they have settled for a unitarianism of the Son, a 'Jesus religion'. And that is not enough, though it is a good beginning.

*Saccidānanda* says to us that you cannot have God or the Absolute without Christ, and that you cannot have Christ without the Triune God. This, of course, is what the western formulation of the doctrine of the Trinity implies. But it is a difficult formulation – three persons (*hupostaseis*) in one substance (*ousia*) – and we have already had some discussion of the difficulty of the term *hupostasis*, and the inadequacy of its Latin translation, *persona*. *Saccidānanda*, when expounded in a Christian way, seems to me to give all the essentials of the doctrine of the Trinity, without using the western terminology.

What is God? 'God is a Spirit, infinite, eternal and unchangeable in His being, wisdom, power, holiness, justice, goodness and truth.' So says the Shorter Catechism. It is not at all a bad description of *Brahman*. The single word *Sat* covers very fully the words 'being', 'goodness' and 'truth'. 'Holiness' is seen especially in the work of the Holy Spirit, and so are power and justice. And 'wisdom' is the Logos, the Word, the *Cit*. Within the Godhead there are essentially the relations of *Cit* and *Ānanda*. God in himself is unmanifest, *avyakta* – the *Deus absconditus* of Luther – but he reveals himself in the Word who goes out, who becomes manifest (*vyakta*), and reveals God to us. God is Holy Power (an expression used by Ninian Smart for *Brahman*),[9] and he is also Love; and that love is revealed in action. The word of love, spoken by the Father, and coming to our world to act and to suffer, is the Son. Like the light and the ray, God cannot remain without communicating himself to us; simply by being, he communicates himself to us through the Word, the Son, the Christ.

### A word for today

Has all this any relevance for our world today? I believe that it has. I have met not a few young people from Europe and America, who have come to India searching for something which they feel the West cannot offer them. Some may be hippies and drop-outs, some may be on drugs. Why are they on drugs? Because they are looking for an experience, for 'kicks', if you like; but really it is for an experience of Reality,

[9] *The Yogi and the Devotee*, p. 45.

of meaning, of the unity of man with the absolute. It is interesting to see what they read: Aurobindo's *Life Divine*; the works of Krishnamurti the theosophist; the delightful and nostalgic yet unsatisfying novel *Siddharta* by Hermann Hesse. In all of these they seek to find an authentic Indian spirituality, the experience of oneness with the universe. And to attain that they reject the affluent society, and choose a life of poverty and wandering – quite in the Indian tradition. The tragedy is that many of them never find what they seek – perhaps because they seek it in the wrong place – and either wreck their lives on drugs or else eventually return to the affluent society and the establishment, and forget the vision and the thirst which sent them off on their pilgrimage. But they speak a word of warning to us; they have found the Church wanting; they have decided that Christianity has nothing to say to them, and that Hinduism and Buddhism are more promising.

And it is at this point that I believe Indian spirituality *has* something to say to the West, and that this quest *can* be satisfied. For we in the West have got away from the peace and joy and rest which Christ can give. We don't have time for contemplation, for letting the peace of God fill our hearts. We have lost the simplicity and the poverty which distinguished Jesus of Nazareth and his first followers. There are not very many Christian centres in India where this kind of life can be found, but there are a few – where the pilgrim from East or West can find peace, and solitude, and perhaps a *guru* who is a fellow-disciple, and who yet has had the experience (*anubhava*) of union with God through Christ, and can speak about it. And the quest will not end with a low-level experience of emotional piety; it will go on, in peace and joy, until the seeker knows that he has found – however briefly – communion with God himself, the Triune *Saccidānanda*. And then, gradually, the will of Christ will become clearer, the word which sends us back into the world, to live not for ourselves, but for him and for our fellow men.

Klaus Klostermaier, a young German who has penetrated deeply into the spiritual life of India, has said that the main concern of India is '*Brahmavidya*' – knowledge of the supreme, union with the Absolute.[10] And our experience of Christ, he insists, must be on the level of that great and supreme experience; no superficial, emotional religion, and no religion of works and rituals can be any good. Christ *is* the revelation of God, and he leads us on to the deepest and highest levels of *Brahmavidya*. India seeks *Brahman*, and if it seeks with total commitment it will be led to Christ. The Indian seeker and the hippy, if they really search till they find, will find Christ, because *Brahman*, the Absolute, the Godhead, can never be fully known without Christ. 'Greek Christology', writes Klostermaier, 'has not exhausted the meaning of Christ, though it has helped the Church the better to see some aspects of Christ. Indian wisdom, too, will not exhaust the mystery of Christ. But it will help the Church in India' – and, one might add, in the western world also – 'to understand Christ better and to let him be really understood: the knowing of Christ as the revelation of the mystery of *Brahmavidya* – Christ, the desire of the eternal hills. . . .'[11]

Those are just a very few of the new insights which Indian Christian theology provides, insights which deepen the quality of witness to the Gospel in India, but which also widen our western understanding. 'One begins to understand the relativity and narrow-mindedness of western theology only after delving deeply into another kind of theology and thereby gaining surprising new insights. And there, too, one discovers Christ.'[12] That is Klostermaier again. In our next chapter we shall take a very basic question: what is the Reality which underlies *all* **our** theological formulations, whether eastern or western? If **these** are different ways of expressing the truth, is there no **way of** penetrating to the Truth itself? What is the Truth behind theology? That is a very big question, and we shall need all the light we can get, from every quarter.

[10] Klaus Klostermaier, *Hindu and Christian in Vrindaban* (1969), p. 108.
[11] *Ibid.* p. 118.          [12] *Ibid.* p. 109.

# 7

# THEOLOGICAL LANGUAGE
# AND THE TRUTH

The motto of the school I attended in Belfast was, and is, *Quaerere Verum*. The search for truth could well have been the motto of Mahatma Gandhi, and in fact he called his auto-biography *The Story of my Experiments with Truth*. His life was devoted to seeking the truth and putting it into action, and for him the word 'truth' was simply another way of saying 'God'. In the *āshram* at Sabarmati, in the suburbs of Ahmedabad, where he lived from 1919 to 1930, there is a large coloured portrait of the Mahatma seated in an attitude of prayer, and below is the inscription 'Truth is God.' It is not a misprint for 'God is Truth.'

The Sanskrit word for truth is *satya*, and this comes from *sat*, which, as we have seen, means 'being', that which really is. *Satya* therefore means 'that which is in accordance with reality'. It also has the connotation of goodness or virtue, as for example in the word *sati*, meaning a virtuous woman, one who immolates herself on the funeral pyre of her dead husband. We should take note also of the word *satyāgraha*, which Gandhi used to describe his campaigns of non-violent resistance to the British *rāj*: its meaning is not 'passive resistance', or 'soul-force', as is sometimes suggested, but is 'insistence on the truth' (*satya-āgraha*).

## The truth behind the statements

Truth, then, is that which really is. We have been talking a good deal about theological statements – the definitions of

87

Nicaea and Chalcedon, of the Westminster Confession, of various Indian Christian theologians, and now we must ask the question, 'What is the truth, the reality behind all these definitions? They speak in different languages – Greek, Latin, Sanskrit, etc. – and come from different periods of history and different cultures, and yet they all seem to point in a certain direction? What underlies them all?

Professor John McIntyre in his book *The Shape of Christology* (1966) has given a very interesting analysis of various 'models' which theologians have used to describe the relation of the Son to the Father – the 'two-nature' model (e.g., of Chalcedon), the psychological model (e.g., of Donald M. Baillie) and the revelation model (e.g., Emil Brunner). He concludes that in all these 'models' we see *human* thinking about God and Christ, representing our partial insights. The definitions of Chalcedon and Westminster are also purely human, and 'do not impose themselves upon us as the dazzling light of truth'.[1] Behind all the models of Christology stands Christ himself; behind all theological models stands God. But the models are human constructions; they are definitely our thoughts, not God's.

Professor T. F. Torrance takes a rather different view from his colleague Professor McIntyre, holding that through the best and truest statements of dogmatic theology – for example the *homoousion* of Nicaea or the Chalcedonian definition – human as they are, we can in fact begin to discern something of the Truth, of the 'shape' of Reality to which they point us. These formulae are, at most, true statements *about* Reality and the Truth, and are not to be confused with the Truth itself. And yet . . . *quaerimus Verum*, we seek the Truth. Is this a possible quest? And can Indian Christian theology give us any help in it? Let us listen to what Prof. Torrance says about the way in which true theological statements are controlled 'from within', as it were, by the very being of God:

Theological formulation takes place through a movement of interpretative and explanatory penetration into the inner intel-

---

[1] John McIntyre, *The Shape of Christology* (1966), p. 175.

ligibility of the divine revelation, in which we allow our human thoughts to be moulded pliantly and obediently by the truth itself, and thus to take their basic form from the inner locution in the very being of God.[2]

In other words, a theologian who is a true theologian will somehow produce theological formulations which reflect the 'shape' of the truth of God. As Prof. Torrance writes again,

The truth of the divine being always breaks through the forms of thought and speech by which we serve it, for it retains its own majesty, freedom and authority over us.[3]

Let us apply this principle to one of the Church's great formulations – the *homoousion*, that is, the dogma that Jesus Christ is of one substance with the Father. This, like justification by grace through faith, is an article by which the Church stands or falls, as much today as at Nicaea or in the notorious Arian controversy of the early nineteenth century. And for the Church in India also the *homoousion* is of vital importance, for there are many who gladly accept Christ as a great religious leader, but deny that he is the full incarnation of God; and many others who would say that he is an *avatāra* of God (one among many, perhaps), but would deny that he is really human. The actual term *homoousion* is very Greek and un-Indian, and is notoriously hard to translate into Indian languages. Yet the truth behind the *homoousion* is essential; only if it is maintained can we solve the great problem which besets Hinduism – the dichotomy between God and the world. For most Hindus, the created world is illusory, is part of the realm of *māyā*; but Christian faith asserts, whatever the terminology it uses, that Christ is the bridge, the link which India desperately needs in order to restore reality and meaning to the created world, and to human life and dignity. The *homoousion* is admittedly not a biblical term, yet in coining it the Church has been allowing 'the biblical

---

[2] T. F. Torrance, 'Theses on Truth', *The Irish Theological Quarterly*, XXXIX. 3 (1972), 217.

[3] *Ibid.* p. 218.

witness to imprint its own patterns upon its mind'.[4] There is, Torrance feels, an 'interior logic' of the apostolic witness, a 'theo-logic' which expresses itself in all theology which is faithful to the Scriptures.

In explaining his theory Torrance places a great deal of weight on the example of modern post-Einsteinian scientific method. The scientist

holds to be true only what he is compelled to think, as he lets the pattern and nature of what he is investigating impose themselves on his own mind. He is not being dogmatical when he does that; he is humbly submitting his mind to the facts and their own inner logic.[5]

The task of the theologian, he holds, is precisely similar:

Theology is bound to its given object, God's Word addressed to us in Jesus Christ. . . . We do not engage in . . . arbitrary speculation . . . but in a thinking that is controlled and tested in accordance with the given facts and their own basic forms.[6]

This means, he points out, that the criterion of truth cannot lie in the interpreter – whether that interpreter be the Roman Catholic *magisterium* or an individual Protestant Bible-student! The centre of authority lies in the truth itself – what Calvin meant by saying that Scripture was its own interpreter, and what Appasamy means when he says that the *śruti* is the primary *pramāṇa*. It also means that definitions or formulae – even that of Chalcedon – are not to be confused with the truth itself. As the Reformers insisted, definitions are fallible human state-ments, and are merely 'symbols' which are always subject to correction in the light of truth itself.[7] Like the pointing finger of John the Baptist in the Grünewald painting beloved of Karl Barth, they draw attention away from themselves towards Christ.

Torrance believes, and I feel that he is right, that in the con-

[4] T. F. Torrance, *Theology in Reconstruction* (1965), pp. 40ff.
[5] T. F. Torrance, *Scientific Dogmatics* (unpubl. MS), p. 2.
[6] *Ibid.*     [7] *Ibid.* p. 3.

text of ecumenical encounter or dialogue this kind of dogmatics – controlled only by the truth and not by any external authority – is likely in the end to lead towards agreement, even, for example, in discussions between Roman Catholics and Protestants.[8] For the closer we approach to the truth, and to the inner 'shape' of the truth, the closer we must approach to our partners in dialogue, provided they have the same quest.

## The need for scientific theology

We must look now at a second point raised by Prof. Torrance, though indeed it is really a continuation of the first. What we need today, he says, is a new kind of theology, a theology which will really be a science, working according to modern scientific principles, and related to post-Einsteinian science instead of to the kind of Cartesian mechanism which still seems to be the background of so much of our present theological effort.

The difficulty is, however, that theology is still dogged by a Platonic, Augustinian, Cartesian dichotomy between what we perceive with the senses and what we know with the intelligence; between the visible, verifiable data of science and our own thoughts about reality; between the world and God. In other words, God and theology have been entirely cut off from the world of science. Science goes its own way, following its own principles, moving in its own closed universe; and God is regarded as being in his own separate universe. And these two spheres do not intersect. It is exactly the same dichotomy that we have seen in Indian thought between the phenomenal world, described as the realm of *māyā*, and the noumenal or 'real' world of *Brahman*. In both western and Indian views this tends to mean that God is separated from the world, and theology regarded by scientists as irrelevant and meaningless.

In the West, this dualism of God and the world came from Hellenism via Augustine. Torrance holds that if theology is to have anything to say in the modern world, it must break away from this dualism, and come to a position where God and the

[8] *Ibid.* p. 5.

world are seen to belong together, so that the theologian can speak of man and his condition, and of the created world; and so that the scientist can do his work within a Christian context. If the universe is regarded as a closed circuit, with no reference beyond itself, then it loses all ultimate meaning. Torrance feels that Augustine is largely to blame for the present state of affairs. The early Greek Fathers, notably Athanasius, had a much more integral conception of God and the world. They stressed the doctrines of creation and incarnation, and saw God as involved in the world, and this gave them a comprehensive view in which God and the phenomena of the world were united in a single whole. Augustine altered all that, and until recently his dichotomy held sway in both theology and science. Today, however, post-Einsteinian science calls for a comprehensive view, with its space-time continuum and the breaking down of traditional barriers between the disciplines.

India too has its great problem of dichotomy between God and the world, and so needs a theology which will give its rightful place to science and will teach a positive doctrine of creation. Recognising this as a fundamental problem for India as well as for western theology, Prof. Torrance writes:

The great problem in the East is precisely this inveterate dualism whether in its Hindu or Buddhist forms. . . . How can this be dealt with in India without thinking through radically the doctrine of creation, and how can we do that without thinking through radically the import of the *homoousion* and 'by whom the worlds were made', that is the relation of incarnation to creation?[9]

So there is our problem, for the West as well as for India: how are we to find the 'shape' of the truth, of reality, if the world and all that is in it is firmly separated from God?

### God and the world

Let us see how the three Indian schools of thought deal with the problem – the *advaita* of Shankara, the *viśiṣṭādvaita* of Ramanuja,

[9] Letter to the author, 20 Nov. 1971.

and Gandhi's *karma mārga* – that is, the three *mārgas* of *jñāna*, *bhakti* and *karma*.

### Shankara

The fundamental principle of *advaita* is that '*Brahman* is true and the world is illusory.' The famous illustration is that of the rope and the snake. You see a snake lying coiled up on the road; when you investigate it more closely, however you find it to be simply a rope. That rope, say the *advaitins*, has three different levels of existence. First – the snake: its existence is purely illusory. Second – the rope: its existence is practical. But the true *advaitin* knows that in reality the rope has no real existence, for it – like everything else – is simply *Brahman*, which alone has real existence. For the moment we shall ignore the lowest level – illusory existence; there remain two levels – the level of ordinary everyday phenomena, and the world of *Brahman*. And between these two there is no connection, no bridge, no way of passing reliably from one to the other. The world of phenomena – that is the world of men, of science, of history, even of the personal God – has no real existence; only *Brahman* is real. The dichotomy is every bit as complete as in Augustine or Plato.

That makes *advaita* look very unpromising as a philosophical system which might help us – as it helped Brahmabandhab Upadhyaya – in formulating Christian theology in Indian terms. Yet it does make two important assertions.

*Saccidānanda Brahman.* First, it asserts that *Brahman*, the Absolute, is essentially triune. And it does this as a postulate of natural, not revealed theology. Aquinas held that natural theology could take us as far as the existence of God, but that revelation is needed to tell us that God is triune. The 'natural theology of Indian religious experience', to use a phrase of Ninian Smart's,[10] takes us straight to the Trinity, although, of course, much Christian exegesis of *Saccidānanda* has to be carried out to give it its full latent meaning. But here, perhaps,

[10] *The Yogi and the Devotee*, p. 13 and *passim*.

we find a helpful clue to something for which Torrance is searching in his new scientific theology. He writes, 'A new kind of natural theology is demanded . . . but not one in which we operate with logical inference from sense-experience to God, for that would involve the mistaken notion that there is a logical bridge between concepts and experience'[11] – that is, the Thomist *analogia entis*. 'We must have a natural theology no longer pursued as a preamble to faith . . . but one brought into the heart of positive theology.'[12] That would appear to be what we in fact find in *Saccidānanda*, and it advances a clear step beyond traditional Christian natural theology. Torrance points out that Augustine, unlike Aquinas, does insist that knowledge of God is basically trinitarian, involving a triadic structure from the first. He feels, however, that Augustine's psychological analogies are inadequate, as the threeness in God is really ontological and not merely subjective, as the analogies imply. It is true that earlier we ourselves noted with approval the parallel between *Saccidānanda* and Augustine's analogy of being, knowing and rejoicing; there is no doubt, however, that from the *advaita* point of view the inner relations of *Saccidānanda* are ontological. Here, then, is a point at which *advaita* can be a useful instrument in demonstrating to us one important aspect of the 'shape' of reality: it is a triune shape.

*Proof by experience.* The second point is this. We cannot prove the threeness of the Absolute either by logic (inference from an established principle) or by analogy (as Aquinas sought to prove the attributes of God *eminenter*, through the *analogia entis*); but *advaita* assures us that we can know *Brahman* by experience. For the *advaitin* such experience is certainly not anything emotional, but is rather a direct intuitive knowledge of the Absolute, often described in terms of identity. To quote Klostermaier, 'We are not concerned with the *concept* of *Brahman*, but with the *reality*. And existential reality can only be grasped in existential experience.'[13] Indian theology always

---

[11] Letter to author.  [12] *Ibid.*
[13] K. Klostermaier, *Kristvidya*, p. 38.

stresses the necessity of first-hand experience. '*Brahman* cannot be recognised through inference of causality (proof of the existence of God) nor through perception, but only through identity,'[14] that is, through the union of the believer with *Brahman*. This too is a vital point: the 'shape' of reality is not something to be speculated about; it is something to be experienced. In the words of the great western *bhakta* Bernard of Clairvaux,

> The love of Jesus, what it is
> None but his loved ones know.[15]

Those, then, are two helpful points from *advaita*. But the problem of the dualism, the dichotomy of God and the world, remains. Brahmabandhab sought to solve it by his exegesis of *māyā* as contingent being; but the 'shape' of his solution was entirely governed by the shape provided by Aquinas, and such a solution does not meet our requirements. We shall return to the subject again after considering the other two *mārgas*.

### Ramanuja

We have already noticed Ramanuja's solution to the problem of God's relation to the world. The world is real, he holds, and it is related to God as body is to soul. This means that (*a*) the world is not illusory, as Shankara held, but also that (*b*) it is not identical with God, as pantheists would claim. Rather it is to be regarded as God's instrument, a body entirely subject to his will.

The objection will immediately be raised that this makes the world co-eternal with God. Appasamy, however, provides a Christian exposition of the idea which avoids this difficulty. He writes:

As a spirit God has no form . . . So He creates the world in order that through it His character may be revealed. The world of

[14] Klostermaier, *Hindu and Christian in Vrindaban*, p. 116.
[15] A better translation is, 'None but who love Him know', from the Latin *Expertus potest credere/Quid sit Iesum diligere.*

physical objects is the instrument by which He makes known His nature and evokes the worship and love of His devotees.[16]

How will this 'model' stand up to scrutiny? It is not very easy to find Scriptural justification for it, though perhaps one could use a passage like Psalm 104. 2, 'Who coverest thyself with light as with a garment.' We find, however, that Ramanuja's teaching on God and the world has two strong points. First, God and the world are kept together in a single 'system', and there is no dichotomy. A single scientific discipline – whether it is natural science or theological science – can explain them both, and at the same time. Physical science is given a real, 'ultimate' meaning. Creation and the body are given their true value. All this would appear to go some way towards meeting Prof. Torrance's requirements.

Secondly, Ramanuja's *bhakti mārga* posits the doctrine of *avatāra* or incarnation, which Shankara's *advaita* will not tolerate. A number of Indian Christian theologians, notably Chakkarai and Appasamy, have given a fully Christian interpretation of the *avatāra* belief, applying it to Christ. (The question does, however, arise, that if God and the world are so closely associated in the 'soul–body model', is there any need in addition for an incarnation?) We shall merely note, at this point, that two such diverse western theologians as Rudolf Otto and Ninian Smart have felt that the *bhakti mārga* provides the closest Indian approach to the 'shape' of Christian reality. Smart writes, 'A natural theology of religious experience seems a necessary aim of Christianity, and in the Indian context finds one supplied in Ramanuja's interpretation of the Vedanta.'[17]

*Gandhi – karma mārga*

Before we return to the unfinished discussion of Shankara let us look briefly at Gandhi's understanding of truth. The two guiding principles of his life were truth (*satya*) and non-violence (*ahiṃsā*). He called truth 'God', as we have seen, but

---

[16] *The Gospel and India's Heritage*, p. 206.
[17] *The Yogi and the Devotee*, p. 129.

never equated *ahiṃsā* with God, presumably because, like most Indian thinkers apart from Aurobindo, he thought of God in terms of being rather than of action.[18] Yet truth and non-violence were so closely linked in all he said and did that it is probably not misleading to say that these two words express his conception of reality. The Indian theologian Nirmal Minz points out that Gandhi's understanding of *ahiṃsā* is deeply coloured by his knowledge of Christ, the great example of non-resisting, self-sacrificing love. Minz writes, 'God in Jesus Christ is outgoing *satya* through the medium of *ahiṃsā*,'[19] and he goes on to say that 'the Gandhian vision points to the ontological relatedness of *satya* and *ahiṃsā* as the basic structure of reality, because they are the converse and obverse sides of the same reality'.[20] We may go on from that to the point which has often been made, that Gandhian *ahiṃsā* is much more than mere non-violence: it approximates very closely to what Christians understand by love – the *agape* of Christ himself. We may say, then, that for Gandhi reality is *truth in action as love*.

### *An interpretation of the Vedantic 'types of existence'*

This Gandhian insight gives us, I believe, a clue which we can now use in an attempt to solve the *advaita* problem of the two dichotomous 'types of existence' – the 'practical' level and the 'real' level – the level of *Brahman*.

The practical level (the word used is *vyavahārika*) is the ordinary level of phenomena, so we can leave it as it is; on this level the scientist – or the theologian – can study, measure, verify the world of the senses. But what about the level of *Brahman*, which is technically called 'the level of supreme meaning' (*paramārthika*)? Can we allow that it is in fact a different level of existence from that of practical life? I believe

[18] I owe this point to Nirmal Minz, *op. cit.* p. 150.

[19] *Ibid.* p. 191.

[20] *Ibid.* p. 192. Compare Erik H. Erikson, *Gandhi's Truth: On the Origins of Militant Nonviolence* (1970), p. 412: *Ahimsa* means 'not only not to hurt [another person] but to respect the truth in him'.

that we can if we are very careful in defining what we mean by reality. For *advaita* the supreme reality is *Brahman*, or *sat* or being, and this implies that the practical and the *paramārthika* levels are ontologically different. What happens if we apply here Gandhi's insight that truth (*satya*) and love are one? Reality then becomes Love, and passes from the realm of being into the realm of action. We shall then find that we indeed have two levels: first the 'practical' level, the level of science, of sociology, of created life; and above that – not ontologically but spiritually and morally – the realm of love, the realm where God is, and where we too can, by his grace, find ourselves.

If we go back, then, to *Saccidānanda Brahman*, we find that it is simply – Love. Reality (*sat*), truth (*satya*) and love (*prema*) are all one. And we remember the Johannine 'God is love' (1 John 4. 16), and Jesus' words, 'I am the truth' (John 14. 6). An Indian theologian, Dhanjibhai Fakirbhai, whom we shall study in more detail in the next chapter, has written:

After pondering deeply on the nature of God, philosophers have said that God is *Sat, Cit* and *Ananda* . . . He is self-existent and eternal; He is conscious, aware and intelligent; and He abounds in joy. But beyond all this we can say something further about God, and that is that He is *Love* – filled with Love, and Himself the very form of Love. This does not mean simply that God *shows* Love, or that He is merely like a loving Father. It means rather that God's very essence or being is Love; His nature is Love. He Himself *is* Love.[21]

What is the bridge between these two realms, which are still separated, though no longer ontologically? The bridge is surely the Logos, the *Cit* of *Saccidānanda*, who proceeds in love from the Trinity, and in love comes to the world of men, to assume their nature, and to change them into his likeness, for 'if any man is in Christ there is a new creation' (2 Cor. 5. 17). In him we see love *in action*, for here being and action are brought together; the Logos comes forth from the being of the

---

[21] Dhanjibhai Fakirbhai, *The Philosophy of Love* (Delhi, 1966), p. 1.

Father to bring the world of men back into the fellowship of love. In the words of Narayan Vaman Tilak,

> So, Love itself in human form,
> For love of me He came.[22]

There are three things to be said about this exposition of *Saccidānanda* and the 'types of existence'. First, I think it brings us rather close to Athanasius, the great Greek theologian of the fourth century. In Prof. Torrance's words, Athanasius 'rejected cosmological dualism and the notion of the Logos as a cosmological principle, for the Christian notion of the Logos or Son by whom God created the universe and through whom he interacts with it in redemption', and then worked out a 'logic of grace', in the light of which he 'expounded the interrelation of creation, incarnation and redemption, and went on to lay the scientific foundation upon which the theology of the Christian Church has rested ever since'.[23] Here too, in this Indian insight, we have the rejection of cosmological dualism and a 'logic of grace' working through the love of Christ.

Secondly, we have discovered here a fusion of being and action. Indian thought tends to concentrate on being at the expense of action, but here, through the outgoing in love of the Logos, we find action linking God and the world. We are reminded of Gandhi's words, 'God appears to you not in person but in action.'[24]

And thirdly, by describing the work of Christ as we have done, we have arrived – as did Athanasius – at the doctrine of incarnation, which is not normally associated with *advaita*. In other words, we have found it necessary to combine features from all three *mārgas* – *jñāna*, *bhakti* and *karma*. I do not think that such combinations can in the end be avoided, though Brahmabandhab tried hard to be a consistent Christian

---

[22] From the lyric, 'One who is all unfit to count/As scholar in Thy school', in *Church Hymnary*, 3rd edn, no. 82.

[23] T. F. Torrance, 'Newton, Einstein and Scientific Theology', *Religious Studies*, 8 (1972), 245.

[24] Quoted in Erikson, *op. cit.* p. 410.

*advaitin.* But today most Christian commentators, for example Appasamy, Dhanjibhai Fakirbhai and Ninian Smart, seem to feel that some kind of interaction between the *mārgas* is both possible and desirable. (Perhaps this gives us a clue to the solution of a problem raised in a later chapter, the inter-relationship of two western *mārgas*, evangelicalism and ecumenism!)

We began this chapter by asking whether or not it was possible to come in touch with the truth, the reality behind all our theological statements and 'models'. Certainly we cannot now produce a formula and say 'this is the underlying reality'. For we are not trying to do what the demythologisers do – to produce a Gospel denuded of its content and reduced to a few abstract principles which have no cutting edge. Anything we can say at the moment must be rather vague and provisional, yet every time a true theological statement is made, and tested against Scripture, it can fill in more details of the picture, like the gradually growing image on a radar screen, or like stereo sound becoming more realistic as more loudspeakers are added in different positions.

The evidence from both India and the West points then to God as triune in his essence.

It points to the Logos, the Son who is one with the Father and one with us.

It points to love in the Godhead, and suffering love in the Son who is the bridge between the world of God and the world of men and things.

It points to changed men and a changed world, as the love of the being of God goes into action in the world of men.

It says that the mystery of God cannot be known by inference or analogy, but only through direct experience of union, and through the testimony of the Scripture.

It says that if we would approach the triune reality we must make our approach through the Son, who first came from the Godhead to meet us and unite us with himself.

That is the barest outline of the truth. But it is a truth which comes ablaze with light from many lands and many ages. For the door is open for many 'models' and for many 'schools' of theology. Only the truth insists that all schools and all models shall conform to Scripture and shall be verified by experience. And it says, 'O taste and see that the Lord is good' (Ps. 34. 8).

# 8

## PORTRAIT OF AN
## INDIAN THEOLOGIAN –
## DHANJIBHAI FAKIRBHAI

In the last chapter we spoke about the truth or reality underlying theological formulations, and also about the need for a
new kind of theology which will take account of modern
scientific procedure, and eliminate the gap between the world
of man and the level of divine activity, a gap which is found not
only in most Hindu thought but also in much western thought
from Augustine to the present day. I propose to devote this
chapter to a study of a single Indian theologian, Dhanjibhai
Fakirbhai (1895–1967). He is not one of the better known
figures, though his works are gradually attracting more and
more attention. There are good reasons for choosing him,
however. His work is a remarkable effort to present the Gospel
in a 'shape' which is at once thoroughly Indian, thoroughly
modern, thoroughly biblical, and wholly based on first-hand
personal experience. That is quite a recommendation! And
secondly, I myself had the great privilege of knowing him and
co-operating with him in some of his work, and so I can commend him as a man and a true Christian *bhakta*.

### *The man*

Dhanjibhai Fakirbhai was born a Hindu in 1895, in the city of
Baroda, and grew up in a devout home, in an atmosphere of
*bhakti*. He absorbed this spirit of personal devotion, especially
from his mother and grandmother. He went to a Christian
school, where his interest in the person of Christ was aroused,

and he began to study religious books, both Christian and Hindu. He tells us how his study and thinking led him one day to an illuminating personal experience of Christ:

Once as I was walking with open eyes over a road the morning sun burst into view behind some houses, and with its sudden light a voice said in my heart: 'Do you seek God? Jesus is God'. This entered into me as a deep conviction and light. Ever since that time Jesus has been to me God, and I have never had to go back on that revelation nor do I need any other God.[1]

As a result of this conviction he decided to become a Christian, and was baptised, and from that time the experience of Jesus as God and Lord became the centre of his life.

Dhanjibhai became a well-known university lecturer in physics, and published a number of technical books in this field, and even in his later devotional and theological writings one is often conscious of his training in scientific discipline and ways of thought. All the time, however, he was deeply aware of his duty as a Christian layman to witness to his faith among his non-Christian friends, of whom he had a great many; and in order to fit himself better for this task he successfully completed an external B.D. course at Serampore University, despite his many other commitments. When eventually the time for his retirement came he gave himself completely to the work of writing Christian books, both devotional books for Christians and also works which in a highly attractive and original way presented the Christian faith to Hindus. It was during this time that I came to know him, and I look back with great pleasure on the many hours I spent with him, sometimes studying the Gujarati *bhakti* poets, sometimes in theological discussion, or working together on some manuscript for the press. He was a tall, stooped figure, a man with gentle manners and a gentle voice, and he gave very freely of his time, his money and his great gifts in the work of producing and distributing Christian literature. He died after a brief illness in 1967, at the age of 72.

[1] *Khristopanishad* (Bangalore, 1965), p. 4.

## The writings

Dhanjibhai's earlier Christian writings were mainly devotional, and not a few of them were translations or adaptations from English. For example he translated Henry Drummond's *The Greatest Thing in the World* (1956) and Stanley Jones's *The Might of Sacrificial Love* (1957). There were a number of books of prayers, including a *Diary of Private Prayer* (*Prārthnāñjali*) not unlike John Baillie's. There was an anthology of Christian poems, some selected from Gujarati Christian writers, some translated by Dhanjibhai from the Marathi, especially of Narayan Vaman Tilak. There was a book called *Premopaniṣad* – 'The Upanishad of Love' – which was an anthology of devotional writing from both East and West, including passages from Augustine, Bernard, Henry Suso, Ramond Lull, Samuel Rutherford, Sundar Singh and Narayan Vaman Tilak. Later there was an allegorical novel called *Ātmakuṅvari*, based on Tennyson's poem *The Princess*, and telling the story of how the human soul resists the love of the princely Son of God, but finally surrenders to his constancy. There was a translation of a life of St Francis. And there was a full-scale life of Christ called *Prāktya* – 'Revelation' – which he left in manuscript, but which has not yet been published. This long list of publications gives us a clear idea of his interests: he was a follower of the Christian *bhakti mārga*, steeped in the devotional heritage of both East and West, and eager to let others share in that heritage.

But there is another group of writings which is more important than these, and in which we see reflected his passionate love of the Bible, his own deep Christian experience and commitment, and his highly interesting attempt to present the message of the Christian faith in a way which would win a response from Hindu readers.

Two of these books are simply arrangements of biblical passages, with no editorial comment at all. *The Draught Divine* (1966) presents the teaching of Jesus. And his most widely circulated book *Shri Khrist Gita* ('The Song of the Lord Christ', originally published in Gujarati about 1955 as 'The Song of the Heart') is a very interesting presentation of the Christian faith in the form of a dialogue between the Lord and his disciples. More than 17,000 copies of this little book have been sold, and it has been translated into several languages. Its 'shape' is that of the most famous of all Hindu Scriptures, the *Bhagavadgītā*, in which there is a dialogue between Shri Krishna and the warrior Arjuna. Some of the topics covered in this dialogue-arrangement of Bible teaching are: the way (*yoga*) of faith, the way of love, of action, of salvation, of knowledge, of sacrifice. Bishop A. J. Appasamy, who wrote the preface of the English edition, says of it that 'many familiar passages in the New Testament will be found to glow with a new meaning in their new setting'. This is a book which has helped thousands to an understanding of the Christian faith.

The next little book I want to mention is *The Philosophy of Love*, published in Gujarati in 1962 and in English in 1966. It is a very brief but concentrated essay, consisting of a mere fifteen paragraphs, and with an appendix containing Scripture proofs, for Dhanjibhai was one who always rigorously applied the test of Scripture to everything he wrote. In the last chapter we quoted a few lines from this book, describing how *sat*, *cit* and *ānanda* are characterised by love (*prema*). In the course of these terse paragraphs we are taken through the whole 'way of salvation', with a distinctive use of Hindu terminology which is both profound and simple.

Then came *Khristopanishad* ('Christ-Upanishad'), published in 1965. (In Hindu literature the Upaniṣads are books which contain in unsystematised form the fundamental teachings of Indian philosophy; they are regarded as part of the inspired *śruti*, and were mainly written before 600 B.C.) *Khristopanishad* is Dhanjibhai's fullest theological treatment of the person of Christ, and of the nature of the life of union with him.[2]

Dhanjibhai's last major theological work – if 'major' is the

[2] An interesting sidelight on the western neglect of Indian Christian theology is provided by Ninian Smart's book *The Yogi and the Devotee*, published in 1968, though based on lectures given in 1964. In it (p. 167)

correct term to apply to something that is very slim in bulk, like most of his volumes – is called *Ādhyātma Darśana* ('A Vision of Spirituality'), and it has not yet been published, although portions of it will appear in a forthcoming anthology of his writings. In this work, finished shortly before his death in 1967, Dhanjibhai adopts a new approach. He had been making a detailed study of the Upaniṣads, and had been struck by many passages which seemed to him to be preparing the minds and hearts of Hindu devotees for openness to Christ. So instead of his usual approach of arranging a selection of passages from the Bible, he here sets out to describe the meaning of Christian spiritual life by the interplay of passages from both Christian and Hindu Scriptures. Nor does he here leave the passages without commentary, as in *Khrist Gita*; they are linked together by his own brief comments, so that we can follow his line of thought. He seeks to show that Christ, as the Logos, is the one who fulfils the aspirations of Hinduism; and he describes union with him as *Khristādvaita* or 'Christ-non-dualism'. We shall return to this term a little later.

### The 'shape' of Dhanjibhai's teaching

First, we have seen how Dhanjibhai tried to present his teaching in a form or shape which would be familiar and attractive to Hindu readers – a *darśana* or philosophical system; an *upaniṣad*; a *gitā* or holy song. (And if a few Hindus objected to this form as a sort of Hindu coating to a Christian pill it was always possible

---

the author expresses the hope that one day some Indian Christian writer will produce a 'Christ-Upanishad', and he proceeds to give a brief outline of what the contents of such a book should be. Obviously Prof. Smart had not read Dhanjibhai's book during the two or three years between its appearance and the publication of his own work, and this is unfortunate, though far from inexplicable, as books published in India are not easy to obtain in other countries. The time is now ripe for Indian Christian theology to claim its rightful place in what Prof. Smart calls 'the interplay between the Upanishads and Catholic theology'.

to remind them that the English version of Gandhi's famous commentary on the *Bhagavadgitā* was entitled 'The *Gospel* of Selfless Action'!) That, of course, is a merely external matter of presentation, but it is not unimportant.

Secondly, we have already noticed Dhanjibhai's firm commitment to the two great *pramāṇas* of Scripture and experience. Everything he writes is controlled by these, and he writes with a most unusual brevity and self-discipline, checking virtually every sentence against the New Testament.

Thirdly, in terms of the three traditional *mārgas*, he is firmly within the *bhakti* tradition, which he inherited from his mother. We see this in a variety of ways, but especially perhaps in his delight in the poetry of *bhakti*, and in his use of the term *avatāra* for incarnation. He does not, however, totally reject the ways of *jñāna* (knowledge) and *karma* (action), and is prepared, as we saw in the last chapter, to integrate them into his general *bhakti* outlook.

Finally, he is also a man of the modern world, a trained scientist, author of a textbook on radio and television! He has a positive outlook on the created world, is familiar with current theory on biology and evolution, and has to some extent been influenced by the kind of biological, evolutionary, eschatological view that we have already noticed in the Hindu Sri Aurobindo and the Christian Chenchiah, and which is best known in the West through the work of Teilhard de Chardin.

Those, then, are some of the factors which give a distinctive shape to Dhanjibhai's theology. We shall now turn to look at his treatment of a few selected points of doctrine.

## 1. *The Trinity*

Writing as he is mainly for Hindus, Dhanjibhai takes a very commonsense, logical and Scriptural view of the Trinity. Here are a few sentences from *Khristopanishad*, and we should try, as it were, to read them with Hindu eyes:

God is spirit. The Holy Spirit is said to be the Spirit of God. Thus God and the Holy Spirit must be one Spirit; there cannot be two Spirits of God or two Spirits in God. The Holy Spirit is said to be the Spirit of Jesus. Now Jesus cannot be two Spirits; there cannot be two Spirits of Jesus or two Spirits in Jesus. So Jesus and the Holy Spirit are one. Jesus said, I and the Father are one. Thus God the Father, Jesus, and the Holy Spirit are one and the same Spirit. God is Spirit and the only Spirit.

Jesus said, 'The Father will come and dwell in you; the Holy Spirit will come and dwell in you; I shall come and dwell in you; abide in me and I in you.' There should be a personal realisation of the indwelling of God as one Spirit. It is for the believer who has this indwelling in him to realise God as one in personal experience, and to have the unified idea of God; otherwise he keeps on oscillating in pluralism. With the clear idea of God the Father, God Incarnate, and God's Spirit dwelling in the heart, everyone should experience in himself the oneness of God. This is a simple thing for a simple man to understand and realise.[3]

That *is* a simple explanation for a Hindu – in fact it is deceptively simple, like much of Dhanjibhai's writing. He describes God in terms of Spirit – *Paramātman*. He stresses 'realisation' – the *pratyakṣa anubhava* of which we have often spoken. The idea of the 'indwelling' Spirit or *antaryāmin* (to use a common term of the *bhakti* tradition) is dwelt on. And at the same time he deals effectively with the unity in Trinity of God: God is Father; God the *avatāra* becomes incarnate; God the Holy Spirit indwells us as *antaryāmin*. Yet we experience God as one. It is not a proof of the Trinity, but a realisation.

## 2. The Incarnate Logos

In *A Vision of Spirituality* Dhanjibhai gives a very interesting, if tantalisingly compressed, account of how Christ the Logos originates from the Father and becomes incarnate. We find him using the 'model' of the sun and its ray, which we saw earlier in the work of the Apologists and Tertullian. Dhanjibhai, however, seems to have discovered it independently from his study of the Hindu Scriptures, for it occurs in the *Brahma Sutra* (3: 2: 18), and from there he quotes it.

For Logos, Dhanjibhai does not use the word *cit*, but two other rather interesting terms taken from the Upaniṣads. One is

[3] *Khristopanishad*, p. 3.

*prajñāna,* which means 'primeval intelligence'. That is, obviously, rather a good word to use for the pre-existent Logos, who 'was in the beginning'; and it is especially suitable as the Upaniṣads equate *prajñāna* with *Brahman* (*Ait. Up.* 3. 1. 2–4). Here is the passage which Dhanjibhai quotes:

That which is heart, mind, consciousness, perception, discrimination, intelligence, wisdom, insight . . . all these, indeed, are appellations of *Prajnana.* He is *Brahman.* . . . All this is guided by *Prajnana,* is based on *Prajnana.* The world is guided by *Prajnana.* . . . *Brahman* is *Prajnana.*

The other term which Dhanjibhai uses for Logos is *Śabda-Brahman,* which means simply 'Word-*Brahman*' or '*Brahman* – the Word'. That too is clearly capable of a deeply Christian meaning.

I shall not attempt to reproduce Dhanjibhai's exact words at this point, as his text is very compressed, and interlaced with quotations from the Upaniṣads and the *Brahma Sutra,* but I shall try to give the gist of his argument in a few sentences:

*Prajnana,* primeval intelligence, is the power which creates, maintains and inspires the world and human beings. *Prajnana* is power and wisdom, is the Word of God (*Sabda-Brahman*), is God himself – *Brahman.* This Word of God, *Prajnana,* took a body in the man Jesus. As the heat of the sun's light, according to the *Brahma Sutra,* is no different from the heat of the disc of the sun itself, so this incarnate *Prajnana,* the *Avatara,* is fully God.

That, I believe, says something which a Hindu can understand, and which – if he does understand it – will take him very close to the orthodox Christian doctrine of the incarnation of the Logos.

## 3. Sin

The vivid consciousness of sin, though it is found in some of the *bhakti* poets like Tukaram, is definitely not a characteristic of the Indian way of looking at things, and indeed many Indian writers, both Hindu and Christian, have been ready to characterise the western preoccupation with sin as morbid. To some extent, though not entirely, Dhanjibhai shows the same tendency. Basically, for him, evil is the negation or absence of goodness, a state of Godlessness. There is no need, therefore, to dispute the question of the origin of sin and evil; they are simply the absence of positive goodness, and so represent the natural, normal condition of man.[4] It would appear that here Dhanjibhai is influenced by the idea that evil is *māyā*, unreal illusion. He writes: 'Darkness has never conquered light. Negation has no power to vanquish that which is real. *What is real has existence; what is unreal has no existence.* . . . God is light and in him there is no darkness at all.'[5] The Christian corollary which he draws from this principle is that where Christ, the true reality, is, there evil or sin, as unreality, can have no standing. 'With the full presence of Christ, Satan gets no place. . . . When life is full of God, Satan does not get a foothold.'[6] I am reminded of a favourite Gujarati hymn, addressed to the Holy Spirit, with four rather vivid and colloquial lines:

> All my sins and all my failings
> In Thy light shall flee away;
> Like wild beasts that prowl at night
> But creep away at break of day.[7]

Actually, Dhanjibhai does in some other places give a more 'western' view of sin (e.g., in *The Philosophy of Love*, para. 5), but it is worth noticing here this 'eastern' (in the sense of Greek as well as Indian!) approach.

### 4. *Suffering Love*
For sheer unadorned and clear Christian teaching, Dhanjibhai's paragraph on 'Suffering Love' in *The Philosophy of Love* is hard to equal. Here is part of it:

The fruits and consequences of man's sinful deeds cannot be cancelled without the performance of atonement and sacrifice.

---

[4] *Ibid.* pp. 36, 37.
[5] *Ibid.* p. 37. My italics.  [6] *Ibid.*
[7] By Kahanji Madhavji Ratnagrahi (1869–1916), tr. W. H. Rutherford.

Forgiveness which does not involve suffering is meaningless and worthless. Man cannot obtain pardon for his sins unless the Divine Incarnation suffers for those sins. And that is the work which the Divine Incarnation carries out through his sacrifice of himself. Here is the great work of God's Love. Every individual who is united with God can obtain the benefit and the fruit of this mighty act. By coming in the form of man and being fully united with man, and for man's sake carrying through this wonderful and fruitful work of atonement (*prayascitta*), God saves man from the fruits of his own misdeeds (*karma*).[8]

Here Dhanjibhai deals with the question of getting rid of sin, but he does not forget that most Hindus are more concerned about the burden of *karma* than that of sin. Atonement is seen both in its literal English sense of at-one-ment with God, and also in its aspect of suffering and self-sacrificial love. Further, this work of atonement can be carried out only by the *Avatāra*, the Incarnation of God. One has to remember that inevitably the English translation misses some of the overtones and implications of the original Gujarati, for Dhanjibhai's writing is primarily Sanskritic in its vocabulary and his use of Hindu terms in a Christian context is very skilful.

### 5. *Khristādvaita*

In his last book, *A Vision of Spirituality*, Dhanjibhai introduces a new term for the relationship of faith-union with Christ – *Khristādvaita*. The term literally means 'Christ-non-dualism' or 'non-separation from Christ'. If we have certain reservations about the term we should remember that although the unqualified word *advaita* (non-dualism) is the term used for Shankara's absolute monism, Ramanuja's personalist *bhakti* is known as *viśiṣṭādvaita* (modified non-dualism), and Vallabhacarya's highly emotional *bhakti* as *śuddhādvaita* (pure non-dualism). Dhanjibhai's coining of the term illustrates his conviction that the Christian life is essentially one lived in constant faith-union with Christ – the union of love, not of absorption. Other terms which he uses to describe the life in Christ are 'the *yoga* of Love', 'spirituality' (*ādhyātmiktā*) and 'God-life' or

[8] *The Philosophy of Love* (Delhi, 1966), p. 7.

'Divine life' – the last two reminiscent of Aurobindo. It is a life which begins with spiritual birth, when the disciple surrenders himself to Christ, and invites him to dwell in his heart.

In his description of *Khristādvaita*, Dhanjibhai is very conscious of the fact that Christ brings unity to the whole world, and in fact he enumerates six different kinds of unity: (i) the unity of the Son with the Father; (ii) Christ's unity with the created world, in the Ramanujan sense that he controls it, and that it is the instrument of his purpose; (iii) the more obvious meaning of the faith-union of the disciples with their Lord; (iv) the mutual unity of the disciples with one another; (v) the coming unity of men of all nations and races in Christ; and (vi) man's unity with nature, in the sense that physically we are part of the created world, and should therefore use it to God's glory, not exploiting it by pollution, erosion and so on. Obviously this very wide understanding of the principle of unity gives scope for an interesting view of man, society and nature, and the controlling factor is that Dhanjibhai sees it all as being centred in Christ; it is in relation to Christ that we are to approach all our problems.

We should not be tempted to imagine that this is a sort of veiled pantheism. It is perhaps more like Teilhard's idea of everything moving towards the eschatological Omega-point of Christ, or Zaehner's conception of the 'convergent Spirit',[9] drawing all things to himself. For Dhanjibhai this 'Christification' – to use Teilhard's term – is never a matter of natural or automatic evolution; rather, every individual must make his own decision for or against Christ, and only when the individual himself lives 'in Christ', himself shares in *Khristādvaita*, can he join in God's great movement towards the day when 'the creation itself will be set free from its bondage to decay and obtain the glorious liberty of the children of God' (Romans 8. 21), and when, according to God's promise, we shall see 'new heavens, and a new earth in which righteousness dwells' (2 Peter 3. 13). The quotations are those given by Dhanjibhai himself.

[9] R. C. Zaehner, *The Convergent Spirit* (1963), *passim*.

One last point here, which sheds light on how Dhanjibhai thought of the Church in this same connection of *Khristādvaita*. He writes, 'When individuals have really become one with the Lord Jesus their relation to one another is that of the members of a body. They all form a body for the Spirit of the Lord.' That, I think, is a typical piece of Dhanjibhai's writing. It is thoroughly biblical, thoroughly evangelical, and at the same time it subtly hints at a Hindu idea with which Hindu readers are familiar – Ramanuja's conception of the world as the body of God. And so Dhanjibhai is able to convey to his Hindu friends some of the true nature of the Christian Church as a community of those who are united to their Lord and to one another, and are his body in the sense that they are the totally surrendered instrument of his will, ready to do his work of love in the world. It is a conception of the Church which, unfortunately, the actual Church too frequently obscures by its lack of love and concern, and its appearance as an institution rather than as the body of Christ.

6. *How the Kingdom spreads*

We have seen earlier how Keshub Chunder Sen gave his own interpretation to some words from the *Chandogya Upaniṣad*, using them as a description of the origin of the Logos. In the Upaniṣadic passage, Being (*Brahman*) is described as thinking within himself, 'I am one: would that I were many.'[10] Dhanjibhai takes the same passage, but applies it instead to the *new* creation in Christ. Jesus, he writes,

did not want to be confined into one body. He wanted to live in a large number of bodies belonging to different persons. This was a new kind of creation – 'I being One I shall be many.' He wanted to multiply himself. This miracle he performed by becoming present in and working through many bodies.[11]

In this way, when a man has Christ living in him, his life becomes 'Christ-living, Incarnate-living, the continuation of the Incarnation of God-in-man'. One by one, he says, Christ-

[10] Cf. *Chand. Up.* 6. 2.        [11] *Khristopanishad*, p. 32.

indwelt individuals take up his service.[12] The continued Incarnation works on the principle of the multiplying of life.

By this the transformation not only of individuals, but that of societies, nations and races is also achieved. The necessary condition is to allow the process to permeate from individuals to groups like the leavening of the whole dough when the leaven is introduced in one place.[13]

Some phrases here may sound strange to us – like 'multiplication' and 'the continued Incarnation'. I do not think we need be afraid of them, however; indeed I am inclined to think that if we paid more attention to them we might be able to give clearer evidence that Christ *is* dwelling in us – both as individuals and as a Church – and that we are living centres of growth, of 'multiplication'.

I have been writing about the work of a man I knew and admired. I must admit that at the time I did not fully understand a great deal of what he was saying. Since his death I have tried to penetrate more deeply into his thought, and it has been a rewarding and enriching experience. For here is theology which is Christian, which is Indian, which is modern. It rests on Scripture, and it rests on experience. And it is not primarily speculative. A good many theologians write in order to impress; Dhanjibhai wrote in order to bring men to Christ.

Some critics might say that he is inconsistent; that although he is primarily a follower of the *bhakti mārga* he yet brings in material from *jñāna* and *karma*; that he is as much influenced by his western as by his Indian studies. Perhaps this is so. Yet he is thinking and writing from within the Indian world; he knows instinctively what will work and what will not, and this gives conviction and persuasiveness to his synthesis.

We shall close this chapter with a few words from the last thing he wrote, *A Vision of Spirituality*. Here is real Christian witness:

God took human form and saved men. He took their sins upon

---

[12] *Ibid.*     [13] *Ibid.* p. 33.

Himself and made atonement for their sins as if they were his own sins. . . . His making Himself fully one with us was his identity, unity, *advaita* with us from *his* side. That opened the way for our identity, unity, *advaita* with Him from *our* side. This can happen by our full surrender to Him.

# 9

◄═══════►

# PARTNERS IN DIALOGUE

Not long ago I was in the departure lounge at Belfast airport. We were sitting quietly talking, like a great many other people. Suddenly we saw a policeman speaking to a group of people on a seat. Then he came to us, and said quietly, 'There's a bomb-scare: please go out through the glass doors and down to the end of the ramp.' Then he moved on quietly but quickly to the next group. There was no panic, no loudspeaker announcement, no rush for the doors. But the message got across!

We talk a good deal about proclamation, and we know that the word 'preach' in the Authorised Version of the Bible comes – via the Latin *praedicare* – from the Greek *kerussein*, which of course means to shout a message aloud, like a herald with his trumpet. That airport incident showed me that the most effective method of proclamation is not always the loudspeaker; it can be the whispered word. And there can be circumstances in which the stridency of the herald's voice, or the sight of his armour, may close the ears of the hearer to his message.

The term 'dialogue' has a good many meanings, and at times it is compared unfavourably with 'proclamation'. Later we shall try to define it, but for the moment let us simply use it to cover any situation where there is a speaker and a hearer, and a word passing between them. And with that very wide definition in mind let us ask ourselves how effective we ourselves – as Christians of a particular culture and tradition – have been in our dialogue with various partners.

### Evangelist or colonist?

In New Testament times the Church very rapidly became indigenous in the lands to which it spread – Asia Minor,

116

Greece, Egypt, North Africa, Italy. Paul stayed two years in Ephesus, but normally his missionary visits were of short duration, and he apparently stayed with friends like Aquila and Priscilla rather than setting up an establishment – a mission compound – of his own. But wherever he went he appears to have mixed fairly freely with the people to whom he was witnessing. Roland Allen in his books *The Spontaneous Expansion of the Church* and *Missionary Methods: St Paul's or Ours?* gave classic expression many years ago to the fact that St Paul was not a colonist but an evangelist. True, he did tell the Philippians(3. 20) that their citizenship (*politeuma*) was in heaven – and Philippi was a Roman colony! But if he thought of them as heavenly colonists he certainly did not believe that they should dig in behind their fortifications and refuse to hold dialogue with the native population. Yet that, unfortunately, is what a great many western Christians have been doing ever since the Portuguese first went to India. We remember the *Padroado* of 1514. Even before that, in 1454, a Bull of Pope Nicholas V to the king of Portugal had urged the colonising Portuguese to 'subdue Saracens, pagans and other enemies of Christ', and the missionaries, supported by the colonial authorities, broke down temples and mosques 'to the glory of Christ'.[1] Such methods brought numerical success – witness the large Christian population of Goa today – but they did irreparable damage to relations between Christians and Hindus.

The early British in India – from 1608 onwards – were merchants rather than colonists. They were nominally Christians, but few of them – few even of their chaplains – thought it necessary to give any sort of witness-in-dialogue to the people of India. There was the external witness of Church-going; there were impressive cemeteries – but little else. The cemeteries are still there, and many a ruined garrison church, mute witness to the failure of colonial Christianity.

Even the missionaries were not without the taint of colonialism. Today it is only too easy to criticise them,[2] but at least they

[1] Quoted by K. Baago in *Inter-Religious Dialogue* (Bangalore, 1967), p. 133.
[2] As Manilal Parekh, Kaj Baago and others have done.

talked to Hindus: some even listened. The Church did take root in Indian soil, but its growth ever since has been hampered by the fact that it has been regarded as something exotic and un-Indian. It has been encapsulated inside a hard coating of western culture (if culture is the right word here!) and therefore a fruitful interpenetration with Indian life has been slow and difficult. People are reluctant to respond to a proclamation which comes from a fortified trading-post, or even from an isolated mission bungalow.

The same thing happened in other colonies. When the colonists were accompanied or followed by missionaries – as in Africa in the nineteenth century – there was a response to the Gospel. But when the colonists or merchants went by themselves or were accompanied only by their own chaplains, it appears that there were three possibilities. You could enslave the local population, or fill the country with your own imported slaves; and slaves would not object to becoming Christian. This happened in the West Indies and in the Southern States of America. Alternatively you could virtually exterminate the native population, as happened in Australia and in parts of America, leaving only a pathetic remnant, with little interest in the Christian faith, and little reason for being attracted to it. Or else you could exploit and antagonise the people of the country, and as it were inoculate them against your faith – as happened very largely in India, China and Japan. For the colonist's main concern is to preserve his territory and his distinctive way of life, not to share them with others. It is a very human instinct – an instinct indeed which we share with the animal kingdom. Konrad Lorenz has some telling things to say about it in his fascinating book *On Aggression*,[3] in which he shows how various kinds of fishes, geese, dogs and other animals will defend their territory or 'biotope' against aggressors of their own species.

Let us take Ulster as an example of one of these colonies. The settlers came, and with them their chaplains. They courageously bore the hardships which face all colonists. They

[3] Konrad Lorenz, *On Aggression* (1966).

did not exterminate the native population, nor did they enslave them. But they failed to share their evangelical faith with them. It is not easy to witness from a walled city to an 'Irishtown' nor even from a fortified farmhouse. The aim of the settlers was to preserve their territory and the rights and privileges and way of life of their community. And that effectively prevented them from the whispered word of dialogue, in which one can share the secrets of one's faith.

And this is perhaps the reason why, alone of all the northern European countries, Ireland never knew the Reformation. Had Ireland not been under British domination in the sixteenth century it is quite possible that an Irish John Knox might have arisen. But when the English in Ireland followed Henry VIII in giving up the Roman allegiance they won no response from the Irish, and it is little wonder that, when later Ulster was 'planted', Protestantism in its Anglican and Presbyterian forms was regarded as a foreign faith – as it still is by the Roman Catholic population. And because the settlers were not evangelists but colonists they failed to cross the barriers and witness in openness and love. They defended their territory and their faith – often very gallantly and often under heavy attack – but they failed in love, and today their descendants are reaping the bitter harvest.

The colonial view of Church growth is part of the Latin inheritance of Christianity. It is true that the Greeks were colonists; yet the English word 'colony' is derived from the Latin *colonia*, which meant an agricultural settlement of veterans on conquered territory acting as a garrison. So far as the spontaneous expansion of the Church is concerned, colonialism has proved sterile. To use the illustration of a modern Japanese theologian, Dr Kazoh Kitamori, it is useless to plant a telegraph pole; what is needed is a living tree.[4]

[4] Quoted in Cecil Hargreaves, *Asian Christian Thinking: Studies in a Metaphor and its Message* (CLS, Madras, 1972), p. 23.

*Crossing the Barriers – the Meaning of Dialogue*

In some quarters today 'dialogue' is regarded as a bad word, whose real meaning is 'parley with the enemy with a view to surrender'. In order to clear our minds of that misconception I think we ought to look at what it does in fact mean. So far as India is concerned, I first began to hear the word 'dialogue' being commonly used about 1959 or 1960, when it became popular through the writings of Dr Paul D. Devanandan, whose book *Preparation for Dialogue*, published posthumously after his untimely death in 1962, is a good introduction to the subject.[5] In the early 1960s a number of meetings for 'dialogue' between Hindus and Christians were held, and I had the good fortune to take part in some of them. Since then the idea and the practice have spread, and 'dialogues' between Christian and Hindu, Protestant and Roman Catholic, have become commonplace.

Dialogue in this relatively new technical sense means meeting someone of a different tradition in an atmosphere of complete openness and friendship, sharing with him your own experience, seeking to share his experience, and leaving the next step to God. Klaus Klostermaier, who has taken part in many dialogues, writes, 'Real dialogues come about when God attracts people to Himself and to one another: it is a communication not of words, but of the Word in one man communicating with the Word in another man.'[6] The same writer says that in dialogue people do not meet 'to talk about religion', for it is not sectarian doctrine or theological theory that matters, but what Indians call 'spirituality' – that is personal experience of God.[7] This kind of sharing demands real discipline, and a real effort to study the other's experience, not just his beliefs read up in an encyclopaedia or a polemical textbook. We have to come with complete honesty, ready to hear God speaking to us through our partner; ready even to change our opinions

---

[5] See also H. Jai Singh (ed.), *Inter-Religious Dialogue*.
[6] K. Klostermaier, *ibid.* p. 125.
[7] *Ibid.* p. 123.

if God should guide us to do so. And yet we do not 'tremble for the ark'; we come trusting in God, knowing that he is truth, and that the truth will prevail. We know that Christ is there with us as we talk, and that when the time comes he will reveal his nature, as he did to the two disciples of the Emmaus road, when they thought together on the Scriptures, and sat together in table-fellowship.[8]

Now let us narrow the scope of our enquiry, and consider in turn three different sets of partners in dialogue.

### 1. *Hindu and Christian*

Dialogue does not necessarily mean a formal, organised meeting. It can have a very simple meaning – a new attitude of openness, friendliness and receptivity to the people of other religions whom one meets. I have often had very useful dialogues on the long railway journeys which are such a feature of Indian life, and they are much more rewarding than the kind of disputation into which it is so easy to be diverted. And perhaps the most effective dialogue is the open and friendly fellowship which a Christian layman can have with his Hindu friend at his place of work, or in his own home, where the effect of a man's faith on his character and 'spirituality' can be observed over a long period.

We mentioned earlier how some thinkers have seen in Hinduism a preparation for Christ. Dhanjibhai felt this about his upbringing, and so does Paul Sudhakar, while Narayan Vaman Tilak said that he had come to the feet of Christ over the bridge of Tukaram. This insight has been given fairly detailed treatment in Raymond Panikkar's book *The Unknown Christ of Hinduism* (1964). His thesis is that Christ has been at work inside Hinduism, though in a hidden way, so that his Name has not yet been revealed there. It is the work of the Christian mission to unveil this hidden Christ, so that Hindus may realise who it is who has inspired all that is best in their

[8] This interpretation of the Emmaus Road incident is J.-A. Cuttat's. See R. H. S. Boyd, *An Introduction to Indian Christian Theology* (Madras, 1969), p. 227.

faith, and so Hinduism itself may be transformed, finding its true meaning and fulfilment in Christ. This theory is essentially the same as that held by Justin Martyr in the early Church, and set forth sixty years ago by Farquhar in *The Crown of Hinduism*.

We do not know how in fact God is dealing with Hinduism, but I believe that through dialogue an opportunity can be provided for Hindu to meet with Christian 'in the cave of the heart'[9] – to use a phrase of Hindu spirituality – and that through such meeting God's will is done, and the way ahead is gradually made clear. Dialogue and witness are not alternatives; it is within dialogue that we can witness most effectively. So, of course, can our Hindu friend. But we are both in God's hands, and he leads in the right path.

### 2. *Roman Catholic and Protestant*

Today dialogue between Roman Catholics and Protestants has become commonplace and no longer excites any special attention. Yet what happens in a situation where Roman Catholics and Protestants belong to two different communities, with different traditions and with rival political and territorial claims – a situation like Northern Ireland? The picture there is a chilling one. Protestant and Catholic both have long and romantic traditions, and are proud to worship as their fathers worshipped; the influence of Calvin, of Aquinas, even of Cranmer, still counts, and counts for a great deal.

Some words of Klostermaier's which I read recently gave me a start when I realised how relevant they were to Ulster: 'Christ comes to India', he writes, 'not from Europe but directly from the Father.'[10] He comes to Ulster not from Geneva or Rome or Canterbury, but directly from the Father. Yet we – and here I speak as an Ulsterman – have sought to keep him to ourselves and to see him only in our own way. It has been such a struggle to maintain territory, to maintain existence

[9] Cf. Swami Abhishiktananda, *Hindu–Christian Meeting Point – within the Cave of the Heart* (Bombay, 1969).

[10] Klostermaier, *Hindu and Christian in Vrindaban*, p. 112.

even, to maintain ways of worship and a way of life. And so colonial Protestantism has been sterile; its culture has been insulated from its surroundings, and has turned in upon itself.

Why did the early Church spread so rapidly? Or Luther's reformation? Or Wesley's revival? It was because the expansion was spontaneous. From the earliest days of the new movement there was a nucleus of indigenous adherents who spread its influence among their own people. But in Ulster there were barriers, the walled cities and fortified farmhouses of the seventeenth-century settlers, the culture bar which still persists. The blame was not all on one side, for especially in recent years the Roman Catholic community remained aloof, opted out of public life, developed separate educational institutions, reacted to oppression with violence. On both sides, those willing to cross the barriers have been few. It is not that there has been any lack of evangelistic activity – on either side. Protestant colporteurs have been unwearying in their task of distributing the Scriptures among Roman Catholics, and in recent years their work has been done in a surprisingly open and dialogue-minded way and has met with a friendly response. And yet . . . While a real reformation is in full swing in the Roman Catholic Church all over the world, Ireland lags behind. Why? The countries where this new reformation has gone farthest and fastest are those where there is openness and friendliness between Protestant and Roman Catholic – Holland, Germany, France, England, the USA. There is good reason to believe that the major impediment to the reform of the Roman Catholic Church in Ireland is the attitude of Ulster Protestants to Roman Catholics. Protestants are preventing the very movement which their faith should above all urge them to promote.

That is one frightening example of what can happen any-where when Christians become so entangled in traditional formulations, structures and attitudes that they lose touch with the Christ who speaks and leads through the Word and through experience – and so lose touch with their neighbour.

In India when Hindu–Christian dialogue is attempted there

is usually a good deal of advance preparation. For some participants there is the prior labour of learning a language; for all there is the attempt to understand, to 'live oneself into' another culture, to listen to what the partner is saying. This discipline is necessary wherever a dialogue is attempted which crosses religious, racial or cultural barriers, and especially where one tradition is in danger of conquest or absorption by another. It is necessary between Roman Catholic and Protestant in Ulster, between white and black in southern Africa; it is necessary in looking to the future of non-European immigrants in Britain. But it is not easy, especially where, as in Ulster, two communities have for centuries rejected each other's traditions, and spoken of 'two cultures' or even 'two races', and where the effort to 'live oneself into' another culture – and above all another 'spirituality' – may be regarded as treachery by one's friends.

If we have dialogue along these lines in Belfast, or Birmingham, or Bombay, does it not mean that my Roman Catholic – or Hindu – friend may convert *me*? Yes, it does. But, as we have already seen, if we join together in seeking, with the help of Scripture, the reality behind all our theological formulations, God will lead us *together* to the truth. My job is not to defend my territory or my privileges, but to share with my neighbour what I have experienced of the love of God.

We must ask ourselves: Are we crossing barriers, or building barricades? Are we a foreign body, to be rejected? Or are we leaven?

### 3. Ecumenical and evangelical

Finally, I want to mention a third set of 'partners in dialogue', whom for convenience we shall call evangelicals and ecumenicals, though we realise that these names are somewhat misleading, and simply represent a general tendency rather than a clearly defined position. But first let us note briefly the significance of what has happened recently in India, with the inauguration there of the Church of North India on 29 November 1970.

On that day in 1970 something really *did* happen (as it happened in South India in 1947). I am a presbyter of a Church which contains former Anglicans, Presbyterians, Methodists, Congregationalists, Baptists and representatives of several more traditions. One legacy of the western captivity of the Church, the so-called 'fissiparous tendency of Protestantism', has been abandoned, and we have found a new and exciting unity, as we have sought to be obedient to Christ's prayer for his disciples that they should all be one (John 17. 21). Here is an impressive fact to set against Lorenz's aggressive urge which everywhere pits man against man in defence of his territory and his rights. It has not been easy to come together, to share one's heritage with others, to give up aggressive and exclusive attitudes, for North Indians are as human as any other Christians. But a way forward has been found, and already it has brought great blessing. The Church of North India still carries a heavy western load – much of it an inherited Latin load – in its doctrine, its worship, its organisation. But at least it has shed the burden of disunity, and that has given it a lighter step.

But now I want to say something about a certain type of polarity which is as familiar in India as it is in Ireland or England, that between evangelicals and ecumenicals. It is a division of western Protestantism which has been becoming more and more pronounced over the past sixty years or so, and it has been exported to the Church in India and other countries. And today, perhaps especially in India, it has hardened and is rapidly becoming institutionalised. On the one hand there is a series of older institutions, supported traditionally and officially by the so-called 'main-line' Churches and missionary societies; they include the Serampore-centred system of theological education, the National Christian Council, the Indian Sunday School Union, the Christian Literature Society, and the Student Christian Movement. In their sympathies these Churches and institutions are associated in a general way with the ecumenical movement. Since the middle 1950s or so the evangelical group has gradually become more and more highly organised and institutionalised, in a series of agencies loosely grouped round the Evangelical Fellowship of India (EFI). In theological education there is the Union Biblical Seminary at Yeotmal, and several other institutions; for students there is the Union of Evangelical Students; in Christian education there is 'CEEFI' (the educational wing of the EFI); and there are various associated publishing houses. Official support for these organisations comes from a number of the traditionally evangelical Churches of European and American origin, and in addition they receive support from evangelically minded individuals and groups within the main-line Churches. Occasionally rather tense situations can arise between adherents of the two *mārgas* – for why should we not use a good Indian word to describe the two 'ways'? – as, for example, when a regional Sunday School organisation decides, after long and heart-searching debate, to change from one syllabus to another.

That is the situation, which I have tried to describe as objectively as possible. I should add, perhaps, that there are many individuals who feel at home in both groups, and do their best to keep them in a healthy and constructive relationship with each other.

And now, at the risk of oversimplification, we must try to identify some of the leading convictions of each of these groups. First of all the evangelicals. In dialogue they would probably make some or most of the following points, as they speak to their ecumenical friends:

(i) You accept critical conclusions on the Bible which for me seem to detract from its inspiration and authority. (ii) You accept conclusions on creation and evolution which similarly undermine the authority of Scripture. (iii) You are unwilling to commit yourself to the penal substitutionary theory of the atonement, which to me is essential. (iv) You seem to me to encourage, or at least to tolerate, various types of radical theology which undermine the faith, especially in regard to the divinity of Christ. (v) You overstress social concern, and undervalue evangelism and conversion. (vi) Your concern for

Christian unity makes you close your eyes to the dangers of Roman claims and Roman expansionism. (vii) Your love for dialogue with everyone could lead you into an uncritical syncretistic world-faith.

The 'ecumenical' in reply will probably say to his evangelical friend something like this:

(i) You close your eyes to the clear evidence of biblical scholarship. This raises doubts about your intellectual honesty. (ii) You also close your eyes to the clear, and by most scientists undisputed, evidence of scientific research into cosmic origins. (iii) The penal substitutionary theory of the atonement – a very western one – is one theory among others. You should widen your conception of the work of Christ, and not include acceptance of a single theory in the conditions of membership of your organisations. (iv) In any 'open' Christian group, radical theology is bound to emerge, but the Church must constantly judge it against Scripture, and 'way-out' movements, like the 'death of God' theology, will soon die a natural death. (v) You understress social concern, for it is in the fields of war and peace, race, poverty, violence that God is calling us to act today. Your evangelism seems to ignore the social dimension. (vi) We are convinced that Christian unity – organic unity – is the will of Christ. We believe that friendly relations with Rome are in fact promoting a reformation within the Roman Catholic Church. (vii) Dialogue is one way of witness, and when we enter it we are in God's hands. We trust in him, and so are not afraid to enter into dialogue with non-Christians.

Those are approximately the two outlooks. And unfortunately each side tends to take up its fortified positions, and all the aggressive instincts come into play, sometimes reinforced by political issues. Where is God leading us in *this* dialogue? It too is one that is vital for the Christian faith.

I think there are several things that can be said. First, the two positions are by no means entirely static, and many people feel that they can subscribe to much on both sides. Recent pronouncements of evangelical gatherings, for example, have shown a high degree of concern for such matters as racial discrimination, poverty and violence. And many well-known ecumenical voices demonstrate their deep concern for evangelism – Bishop Lesslie Newbigin, for example, in the Indian context. Even in the fields of biblical criticism and the doctrine of creation the position is fluid, and there is no level of uniformity among evangelical scholars. We have seen also how a leading evangelical like Paul Sudhakar is prepared to express the Christian faith in terms borrowed from Hinduism. And there are many aspects of Christian life in India, for example, where evangelicals and ecumenicals co-operate very happily – in certain aspects of theological education, in evangelistic campaigns of various kinds, in relief work, and in the fields of education and medicine.

Secondly, there are certain matters which are vital for *all* Christians, although different people may give them different emphases. We should include in them the two primary *pramāṇas* – the absolute necessity of making Scripture our rule of faith and practice, and the need for every Christian to have a first-hand personal experience (*anubhava*) of God in Christ. We should also add social concern, for this was a priority of Jesus himself. In modern Church history it was evangelicals like Wilberforce who first awoke the Christian conscience in this matter, and it should not be neglected by modern evangelicals.

Thirdly, surely it would be a good thing to follow the Hindu tradition here, and simply accept the fact that there *are* two different *mārgas* – the evangelical corresponding not a little to the way of *bhakti*, and the ecumenical appearing sometimes to concentrate on action (*karma*) and sometimes on knowledge (*jñāna*). The Roman Catholic Church has its various Orders, which differ very widely in outlook yet do not affect the unity of the Church. These two great *mārgas* of Protestantism should be able to co-exist without threatening our unity.

Fourthly, and following on from that, is it not better for both *mārgas* to take their place fully within the life of the Church – not only the local, national or denominational Church, but also the world Church, as it is reflected in the ecumenical movement and particularly in the World Council of Churches? To take an Indian example, there have been many evangelicals who have honestly opposed the formation of the Church of North India. Now that the Church is there, however, they are finding that their witness and their special emphases are welcomed, and they can be themselves, and make their distinctive contribution more effectively from within the new Church than they could have if they had remained outside. There are many evangelicals who do make an effective witness from within the ecumenical movement, but there are others – and they are fairly vocal – who devote a great deal of energy to a sterile effort to oppose the World Council of Churches; energy which, if it were devoted to an evangelical witness within the Council might do much to bring new life and enthusiasm and Christian commitment to the whole ecumenical movement and the Churches associated with it.

Finally, this is surely a situation where we are called to show love and understanding and openness. It is a situation of vital importance to the future of the Church and of the Kingdom of Christ. And here above all dialogue is needed; not argument, nor aggression, nor a retreat behind defensive positions. Dialogue seeks to bring mutual understanding, and then to lead *on*, beyond all our positions, governed as they are by traditions and formulations and private opinions, on to God's truth and reality, where those who are wholly committed to him find their unity – in Christ.

# 10

## THE WAY OF FREEDOM

The West has become very conscious of India. Indian music has become popular; so has *yoga*; so have Indian clothes and fabrics. People practise 'transcendental meditation'. In many cities of Britain, America and Australia young people join the Harekrishna cult – a movement with a remarkably high ideal of non-violence, self-control and concern for others. Television programmes promote nostalgia for the British *rāj*. In Britain many thousands of immigrants have brought two cultures into contact in a new and very interesting encounter whose final outcome no one can forecast. At the same time hundreds of young people, hippies and others, make their way to India and Nepal, all seeking for something, though many of them may not be at all sure what it is they seek. It may be freedom from western society with its affluence and its organisation; it may be the experience of unity with the Absolute, an experience which some try to anticipate through the use of drugs, while others genuinely seek to learn Indian techniques of meditation. But the movement is significant. It shows that many young people of the West have failed to find peace and satisfaction in the religion and culture of their upbringing, and have turned to India, subtly attracted by its ancient spiritual tradition. India today can speak to the West, and the West is ready to listen.

This is a book about India. Yet in writing it I have all the time been uncomfortably aware of the explosive political situations in other countries, such as Northern Ireland, Rhodesia and South Africa, Israel and Egypt, and of racial conflicts in America and racial tensions in Britain, of frightened

Jews and Christians in Russia, of neglected aborigines in Australia. Yet primarily I have been conscious of the suffering and fear and misunderstanding in the city where I was born and grew up – Belfast. Can India and Indian Christians give any message of hope in a frightening and depressing situation? If there is a message and if it is relevant to other situations outside Ulster, so much the better.

In this final chapter we shall look first of all at India's doctrine of the secular state, and then go on to draw together some of the lines of thought we have been following.

## 1. *Freedom and the secular state*

Years of living in Ireland and in India have convinced me of the fundamental necessity of the secular state if there is to be real freedom for men of all faiths. The Indian Constitution gives to all Indian citizens the right to practise and propagate their religion; and although the country is predominantly Hindu there is no state religion, nor is the Hindu faith accorded preferential status. Christians and Muslims are well aware that India's commitment to the ideal of the secular state is vital to their welfare, and have gladly supported those like Jawaharlal Nehru and Indira Gandhi who have upheld this policy against parties such as the Jan Sangh who would prefer to introduce a 'sacral society' – in Harvey Cox's phrase – and make India a Hindu theocratic state as Pakistan is a Muslim one. It is significant that the newly independent country of Bangladesh has chosen to follow India's example in establishing a secular state in place of the previous Pakistani theocracy.

If the doctrine of the secular state is right in India and Bangladesh, surely it should apply also in Ireland – and for that matter in Britain. (Ireland at least does not have an established Church, though in the Republic the Roman Catholic Church is at present accorded a special position by the Constitution. England, Scotland and Wales would do well to face and resolve this issue, for in the multi-racial and multi-religious society of today the idea of an established Church is difficult to justify.)

The way ahead in Ireland as in India, would seem to lie in the establishment of a truly secular state, with political parties organised on non-sectarian lines, and with membership open to men of all faiths. Freedom, whether it is in India or Ireland, demands a secular state, and a complete break from the Constantinian, Caesaropapist, Genevan, Elizabethan tradition. Theocratic states, acts of uniformity, and links between political parties and Roman Catholic or Protestant traditions are clearly contrary to the will of God for our time, and should be abandoned.

We have been at pains all through this book to stress the need for Scriptural authority for our theological statements, and it may perhaps be objected here that the evidence of the Old Testament is strongly in favour of a theocratic state, for there is no doubt that Israel was a thoroughly sacral, theocratic society. As Kaj Baago has pointed out, however,[1] the pattern seen in the New Testament, especially at the period of the Pauline epistles, is much closer to the secular state than to a theocratic one. With the spread of the Imperial cult there came times of terrible persecution for the Christians, but in the early Pauline period Judaism (which from the Roman point of view at that stage included Christianity) was a *religio licita*, and it was against that background that Paul wrote Romans 13. The Imperial cult, and the persecutions which accompanied it, were a perversion of the earlier Roman secular state, and it was a great misfortune for the Church that Constantine chose to Christianise the imperial pattern of the sacral society rather than giving to all citizens – including the pagans – the freedom of a secular state. Paul knew that it is better to suffer than to inflict suffering, to be persecuted than to persecute, to be a slave rather than to be a master. That was the belief of the New Testament Church. Christians today should, indeed, take part in politics, and the Church has a prophetic ministry to speak out against all injustice and oppression. But

[1] In *Inter-Religious Dialogue*, pp. 128ff.

that is a very different thing from becoming linked to a political party or a government, for as soon as the Church forms such links it loses its freedom, and runs the grave risk of serving men – even of serving Satan – rather than God. Here, surely, is a place where, in the interests not merely of common justice but of the freedom of the Church, it is better to side with the Anabaptists, with the Quakers, even with the French and Russian revolutions, rather than with Constantine, with the Holy Roman Empire, with Calvin and with the defenders of established Churches.

## 2. *Freedom for openness*

We have seen how the aim of a group of colonists is inevitably the preservation of their own identity, and how this fact isolates them from the surrounding communities and makes the task of effective Christian witness very difficult. As a result one finds, in Ulster for example, polarised communities where there is little opportunity for communication across the barriers. This situation is very far removed from the New Testament ideal of leaven and seed.

Unfortunately the Church in India also has been deeply affected by communalism, in this case partly at least a result of the carrying over into the Church of the traditional caste-structures of Hinduism. And in India, as in the West, communalism can be fatal to the Church's task of witness and service. M. M. Thomas feels that the Indian Church must break away from this communal pattern if it is to become really effective in its witness and service, and his words apply to the Ulster situation also:

We have to find [he writes] a more proper form for the Church in India than the very unsatisfactory form of an Indian religious community [by which, of course, he means a communal group. He continues.] . . . The goal should be the community's capacity to witness to Christ as Saviour, servant and Perfecter of all men not merely as isolated individuals, but as persons in and with their various secular and religious group-ties.[2]

[2] M. M. Thomas, *Salvation and Humanisation* (Bangalore, 1971), p. 60.

But how is the Church to break away from these bonds of communalism? It is not an easy task, whether in India or in Ireland, for people are quick to take up defensive attitudes, quick to defend their frontiers and their privileges, and unwilling to invite others to share in their fellowship. We desperately need to turn from being a closed community to being an open fellowship, ready to serve, to witness, to share with others what we know by experience of the love of Christ and the power of the Spirit; and ready also to share with others our cherished heritages, and especially any rights and privileges which we may have and they have not. This does not at all mean that we must reject the historic Christian Church, as Charles Davis and Kaj Baago have done. But it does mean a readiness to criticise and if necessary to abandon historical structures which have ceased to be helpful, and a readiness to return to the pattern of fellowship-groups of people who have direct experience of God in Christ, who have received the power of the Holy Spirit, who are committed to one another, but committed also to live not for themselves but for others and for God. The Church for so long has been so busy saving its life that it has come perilously near to losing it.

### 3. Freedom to be one

The Christian unity which has found expression in India in the Church of South India and the Church of North India has a very important and hopeful message for the West. Here is a major reversal of the 'fissiparous tendency of Protestantism'. From the Indian point of view the denominational structure of Indian Protestantism was a historical accident, an importation from the West with no historical roots in India, yet it has not been easy for Christians to accept God's gift of unity, and many hindrances have had to be overcome. It can, of course, be pointed out that the Plan of Union of the Church of Northern India, for example, is itself a very western document, and this is true; a western remedy, as it were, has been used to heal a western disease. Yet there is more to it than that. The pressure and urge for unity arose from the Indian situation, and the Church which has now come into existence is an Indian Church moving, like the Church of South India, towards a future which may well diverge more and more from the culture-conditioned patterns of western Churches, while yet remaining true to the Scriptures and to the substance of the faith. Already something *new* has come into being. Many of the features of the new Church are still undeniably western, yet its future development will be increasingly Indian. And already, simply by the fact of its existence and its unity, the CNI has set an example which the West must try to follow. Like the CSI, the CNI has cordial relations with the Syrian Christians of Kerala, especially the Mar Thoma Church, and this points to a fruitful future relationship with the 'Eastern' tradition. Already the use of the well-known 'kiss of peace' in the communion service is an indication of some of the riches in which the new Church may expect to share.

So far as Protestant–Roman Catholic relationships are concerned, the question of unity does not at the moment arise, although the question of dialogue does. The barriers to unity here are fundamental ones, which truth forbids us to ignore or to minimise, the most fundamental of all being the question of the ultimate seat of authority, and especially the relation of Scripture to tradition. There can be no question here of a 'plan of union'. But the quest for truth is an enterprise which can be carried out together – the common search to know God's truth as revealed in Scripture, confirmed by the Holy Spirit in experience, and illuminated (or perhaps obscured!) – by the conflicting traditions of men and of the Church. We believe that when in complete dependence on God and his Word we carry out such a search together, he gradually reveals to us the 'shape' of that truth, and so we are brought closer to one another as we approach closer to the Centre, the Truth, the Christ.

## 4. Freedom for the new

We have examined a number of interesting concepts from Indian Christian theology – the *pramāṇas*, the meaning of *bhakti*, the fourfold ideal of *mokṣa*, the Trinitarian implications of *Saccidānanda*. We have also looked at the main outline of the work of one theologian, Dhanjibhai Fakirbhai, and seen his very helpful and comprehensive conception of *Khristādvaita* or faith-union with Christ. Dhanjibhai, like the other better-known writers whom we mentioned, was seeking to express his Christian faith in the Indian terms with which he and his readers were familiar, in order that Christian witness might become more effective in India. Yet what he wrote is of concern to us in the West. For Indian theologians today are working out the basic issues of theological formulation and vocabulary, just as they were worked out in the early Church by the Apologists, Tertullian and others. The vocabulary which Tertullian evolved has survived in the West till our own day, and will no doubt survive for many centuries to come. Yet it will not work in India, for India cannot go on for ever using a theological vocabulary mediated through Latin via English, and indeed in every Indian language the vocabulary of Christian theology has been evolving steadily for more than a century – in some places for much longer, and is already rich and effective. The continual process of forging a Christian vocabulary for this vast cultural complex is one of the most important and challenging tasks facing Christian theologians today, and one whose progress the western world cannot afford to ignore or underestimate.

## 5. Freedom to retain

Does this 'freedom for the new' mean that we are now free to discard the whole body of traditional Christian doctrine and start again from scratch, as it were? Some radical theologians today would have us believe that this is so, and that dogmatic theology has become nothing more than an expendable burden.

Here is how Kaj Baago puts it, in the context of how secularisation has liberated men from many of the traditional religious sanctions:

Secularisation will free us . . . from that doctrinal system which is called 'the Christian faith'. In this age of science and technology, the creeds and confessions of Western Christendom with their doctrines of Trinity, Incarnation, Virgin Birth, Ascension, Justification, Atonement etc., simply give no sense any longer, not only because they are filled with outdated Greek philosophy and Roman law, but also because they have as their basis a metaphysical world view which nobody can take seriously today . . . We shall simply have to discard these words and this way of thinking theologically, and we shall have to try to build up a completely new theology, which is meaningful in an age of H-bombs and spacecraft.[3]

I think it will be clear from all that has gone before that we cannot accept Baago's sweeping statement that western theological doctrines 'give no sense any longer'. We have criticised the language and the thought-forms of western theology, but we have also made it clear that formulae such as the *homoousion* stand for the truth – a truth which can be expressed also in the idiom of Indian languages and thought-forms. It is our thesis that when a theologian from a non-western culture, for example India, begins seriously to write theology from the basis of the Scripture and his own experience of God in Christ, and when he writes with the use of terms derived from his own cultural background, he will, through the power of the Holy Spirit, be able to describe truly the 'shape' of the truth, of the reality which is the triune God. This does not mean that he should ignore the findings of western theology; they will, indeed, be a useful yardstick for him to assess his work, and for the *oikoumene* to judge it. But he should not allow himself to be diverted by western formulations from finding the word which will speak to his own people in their own cultural surroundings, and bring them to the heart of the mystery of God.

Theologians cannot afford to ignore the lessons of the past,

[3] In *Inter-Religious Dialogue*, pp. 136, 137.

as they cannot afford to ignore the lessons of the world-wide Church. The study and understanding of the Church's traditions are essential, as is the study of traditions other than one's own. The two primary *pramāṇas* are indeed Scripture and experience, but *anumāna* or inference is not to be neglected – that is the Church's traditional teaching, as well as the teachings of the different great theologians and their schools. Serious Indian theologians will not ignore the early Fathers, the mediaval synthesis, the great insights of the Reformation. There is much here that must be retained. Yet Indian theologians have already formulated, and will continue to formulate their own new tradition of dogmatic theology, which must be compared with, but not judged by the theology of the western and Greek Churches, just as their theology must be subjected to the comparison of Indian standards. But the ultimate criterion is not any human or ecclesiastical subordinate standard of West or East; the ultimate criterion is God's truth speaking in Scripture.

### 6. *Freedom to be ecumenical*

That brings us on to another important principle, namely that the Church is a world-wide Church, and that it is at our peril that we limit ourselves to a single cultural context and ignore the *oikoumene*. We have talked a good deal in these pages about the Indian Church and Indian Christians and Indian theology, and we must recognise frankly that there is a danger here – the danger symbolised by the term 'German Christians', used for those people in the German Church in the time of the Nazis who were prepared to accept Hitler's racial theories and his claims to the spiritual leadership of the German people. Some of the Indian theologians of the 1920s and 1930s did, perhaps, go too far in their desire for an Indian Christianity which should have no kind of continuity with the western Churches. Many passages advocating this view could be quoted from the works of Chenchiah or Manilal Parekh; yet that was a very natural reaction against the European-dominated Christianity of the time, and today most Indian theologians have passed beyond this stage to a more universal outlook. The Church in any country should be itself, and should not be too closely tied to external traditions or authority; it should – to use a word which has recently become fashionable – be aware of its own 'selfhood', its own identity in the context of its cultural surroundings.

Yet the Church in any land must be conscious of the rest of the world, of the *oikoumene*, for the Church of Christ is a fellowship which transcends space and time, and international, cross-cultural contacts provide great enrichment.[4] In the past the traffic has been mainly one way – from the West to India – but today there is no reason why this should continue to be so. So far as India is concerned, the classical era of western missions is rapidly drawing to a close, and the number of western missionaries who go there in the future will probably be small. Yet it is important that a two-way traffic should continue, and that we in the West should now take every opportunity to draw on the rich treasury of Indian spirituality and thought, just as the Indian Church has drawn on ours in the past.

It is dangerous for a Church to become too local and introspective, whether that Church is western or eastern, and so to miss the universality of the Body of Christ. Swami Abhishiktananda writes:

The Church is indeed the ferment which transforms . . . civilisations and cultures; but while spreading into the whole dough she is always in danger of identifying herself so much with the dough that at times she seems even to lose her distinctive character. The identification of Christianity with one particular culture in which it developed during its first two millennia prevented Christians from hearing the call of the prophets and the New Testament to universality.[5]

We might add that to limit Christianity to Indian culture would be just as dangerous as to make the identification with

---

[4] Cf. D. T. Niles, *Upon the Earth* (1962), pp. 170ff.
[5] In *Inter-Religious Dialogue*, p. 80.

western Christendom. International, inter-cultural fellowship is of the greatest importance to the Church. We in western lands need the Indian Church and its insights. Perhaps India still needs ours. And we both need the kind of wider fellowship which is found in the ecumenical movement.

The mission of the Church is *one* mission, and it does not matter who is the sender and who the receiver. To cut ourselves off, however, for either nationalistic or theological reasons, from the wealth of fellowship, of diverse traditions and of theological stimulation which is ours in the international, interracial, inter-confessional, inter-traditional fellowship of the ecumenical movement would be a tragic curtailment of the fulness of the Gospel. 'The holy Church throughout all the world' is one, and it is not complete if the contribution of any one Church or culture is omitted from its total. We ourselves in the West are the heirs of many traditions – Jewish, Greek, Latin, Celtic, Anglo-Saxon, German, French. Today the Indian Church is offering its contribution, and we must not only be aware of it, but accept it with joy.


### 7. *Freedom to be evangelical*

When we went into the question of the origins of dogmatic theology we discovered that the two main factors which stimulated men like Justin and Tertullian were evangelism and the refutation of heresy. Theology arose out of proclamation as these men sought to commend their Lord and his work to those around them, interpreting the Scriptures in the light of their own experience of Christ and in the context of Graeco-Roman culture. And still today all true theology must have evangelism as its aim – the sharing of the *euaggelion*, the good news of what God has done for men in Christ. We have seen how clear this aim is in the work of Dhanjibhai Fakirbhai and Paul Sudhakar, and many more. It is an aim which is not in conflict with dialogue; rather, dialogue gives the opportunity for the Gospel to shine in its own light, unobscured by human arguments and 'rational refutations'. In dialogue we seek to make ourselves channels for the grace of Christ and the love of God and the fellowship of the Holy Spirit, as we witness to the newness which comes to those who live in Christ by the power of the Spirit.

Theology can easily become a speculative exercise or even an intellectual game. It can also become sociology or anthropology. The Indian perspective is a good correction here, for in India no man can claim to be a theologian who is not also a *bhakta*, one with direct, unmediated experience of God to which he can bear witness. And a theologian who has had such an experience must bear witness to it, though at times the Indian witness may be somewhat quieter, more subdued than its western counterpart. (We fail to realise, sometimes, that Paul did not in fact say, 'Woe is me if I *preach* not the Gospel' (1 Cor. 9. 16). He really said, 'Woe is me if I do not evangelise.' Even the Vulgate gets this right – *vae enim mihi est, si non evangelizavero*.) The important thing is to share the good news with others, and this may be done in a variety of ways. If we fail to do this we fail as Christians, and fail as theologians.

### 8. *Freedom to be 'human'*

It may seem strange that in a book about India we have said so little about India's vast practical problems – about the standard of living, about the population explosion, about disease and illiteracy, about refugees, relief work and economic development. That is not because these matters are not of vital importance.

Jesus came to bring freedom – 'to proclaim release for prisoners . . . to let the broken victims go free' (Luke 4. 18 NEB). He brought freedom from sickness and death; he brought freedom from sin and the fruits of sin (*karma*); he brought freedom from the bondage of the law. And God gives other freedoms. He brought political freedom to the Jews at the Red Sea and again in the Babylonian exile. He brought religious freedom to Daniel in the lions' den. He brought economic freedom to the poor and the exploited through the prophet

Amos. He brought racial freedom to the gentiles when Jesus broke down the middle wall of partition between them and the Jews. And all men are summoned in Christ into the 'glorious liberty of the sons of God' (Rom. 8. 21).

In Sanskrit *mukti* and *mokṣa* mean 'freedom'. They also mean 'salvation'. Appasamy has explained how for Christians the true meaning of *mokṣa* is union with Christ by faith. And 'if any man is in Christ, he is a new creation' (*kaine ktisis*, 2 Cor. 5. 17); we become new men, real people, in him. This means that in Christ freedom, salvation and new humanity are synonymous.

M. M. Thomas in his recent book *Salvation and Humanisation* (1971) deals with a topic which has been much discussed recently in ecumenical circles. At the Uppsala assembly of the WCC, for example, delegates were divided between the more evangelical, who thought of the mission of the Church primarily as the proclamation of salvation in Christ, and the more radical, who felt that the Church's primary duty today was to identify itself with the world and participate in the world's struggles 'for human rights, social justice, and world community',[6] and so laid their chief emphasis on man's search for true manhood – for 'humanisation'. Out of this a heated debate developed, and there were accusations that anthropology was being given greater importance than theology. I do not intend to go into the debate, which will no doubt continue. I do believe, however, that M. M. Thomas is right in seeing that the solution lies, not in anthropology, nor even in 'mere' theology, but in Christology. Jesus is the true man, the free man, the God-man in whom alone man can rise to his full dignity; and Jesus *does* send his followers to heal the sick, feed the hungry, clothe the naked. But at the same time he calls men to union with himself, to that *mokṣa* which is not only freedom, but also salvation. And wherever his followers may live, in Bombay or Belfast, he gives them the command to offer this freedom, this fulness of life, to *all* men without distinction. We must claim *no* privileges for ourselves which we will not

[6] *Salvation and Humanisation*, p. 3.

extend to all our fellow men. As Dhanjibhai reminds us, union with Christ in *Khristādvaita* involves us not only in unity with our fellow Church-members, but with all mankind. And this will involve us in relief work in Bangladesh, in agricultural projects in Gujarat, in industrial reconciliation in Durgapur, in community projects in Bradford – and in crossing barriers of fear and hatred in Belfast.

## 9. *Freedom and the Latin tradition*

It may seem as though we have concentrated too much in this book on the Latin aspect of our present western theological patterns of thought and vocabulary. Yet it is important that we should isolate and identify this particular feature of European, and especially of English-speaking theology, for there can be no doubt that the English-speaking world reads its theology through Latin-tinted spectacles, whether that theology be Protestant or Roman Catholic. This fact accounts for some strange associations; it demonstrates, for example, that over a very wide range of theological doctrines a Protestant extremist like Ian Paisley stands firmly alongside Thomas Aquinas, with whom he shares a very considerable vocabulary, and a thoroughly Latin and legalistic way of looking at things. After all, from the point of view of a theologically minded Hindu turning sympathetically to the study of the Christian faith, the differences between Rome and Geneva are comparatively minor ones – less divisive, perhaps, than those between the schools of Shankara and Ramanuja. An Indian perspective on the Latinity of our theological vocabulary and ideas makes us aware of how much common ground there is between Roman Catholics and Protestants, and how deeply both our traditions are infected by the spirit of legalism, and the unseemly dedication to structures of power; it should also make us aware that neither of us is really equipped to bear witness in a world of many cultures to the universality of the faith which we have persistently restricted to our own small so-called Christendom.

The great Greek theology of the early Fathers has always acted as a healthy corrective to the Latinity of the West, yet far too few in the West have paid sufficient attention to it. And now a third perspective – that of India – is being added, a perspective which represents the seeking after Christ of a whole great cultural tradition quite different from that of the Graeco-Roman world. I understand that in map-making it is important to take three compass-bearings in order to verify the position of one's objective. In theology we in the West have been far too ready to define the truth simply according to our own Latinised standards. A few scholars with a special interest have paid some attention to the Greek Fathers, and to modern Greek or Russian theologians. Surely the time has now come when, with the aid of Indian theology, we should seek to come to a clearer, more definitely fixed, more three-dimensional understanding of the truth. As Chenchiah once wrote in support of the claims of Indian theology,

If it be said that by the time of the Nicene Creed all the factors of the faith, East and West, have been brought together and faith become complete, my answer would be that . . . by virtue of India's pre-eminence in religion, it cannot be said that all the factors of common faith have been assembled without her contribution. Even if a common faith could be evolved without her, it cannot be completed without her contribution.[7]

The Christian faith does not, of course, depend finally on any theology, for all theology is an attempt to define and explain what God has given to us in Christ. Yet surely Chenchiah is right in believing that today, when a world-society, a real *oikoumene* is a reality, it is presumptuous to assume that we can carry out our theological thinking in total isolation from one of the world's major cultures. By widening the range of the cultural context of Christianity we are not simply helping the work of Christian witness in India; we are correcting and deepening the scope of ecumenical theology.

[7] P. Chenchiah, in Madras *Guardian*, 30 Jan. 1947.

## 10. *Freedom for the truth – Satyāgraha*

Truth was the passion of Gandhi's life, and for India truth (*satya*) and reality (*sat*) are one. All our theology is an effort to penetrate to the truth behind the formulations – to *find* the one whom we and all men 'feel after' (Acts 17. 27 AV). And India tells us that this must mean *realisation* – not mere intellectual apprehension. 'You shall know the truth, and the truth shall set you free,' said Jesus (John 8. 36), and he himself is that truth (John 14. 6). The task of our theology, then, is to reach the 'shape' of reality and truth to which the Scripture and the tradition point us, and that shape is the form of the triune God, revealed in Christ the truth.

But how are we to find the truth? In the West, theologians have been far too ready to make this an intellectual matter, a search for 'orthodoxy', for right beliefs. One of the greatest tragedies of the history of dogma is that we have so often concentrated our attention on our orthodoxy and the preservation of our ecclesiastical structures, and have forgotten the transforming power of the Holy Spirit. For without the power of the Spirit we cannot know the truth, and so cannot experience freedom. India has not neglected the things of the Spirit, but has tended to look only within. The message of Pentecost is that reality itself, truth itself, the very triune God himself sends his Spirit to lead us into all truth. 'When he comes who is the Spirit of truth, he will guide you into all the truth' (John 16. 13 NEB). Here is the secret of freedom – the power of the Spirit.

Again and again we have noticed Indian Christian theologians speaking of the Spirit, and from time to time we have used the word 'spirituality' – a word which sounds rather pretentious and even precious in English, but which is so natural and so familiar in the Sanskritic languages. It was through the Spirit, we saw, that Nehemiah Goreh came to understand the meaning of the Trinity. For India lives in the realm of the Spirit, the *Paramātman*; and the doctrine of the Spirit is a natural place to begin one's theological construction.

In the West today we speak much of humanity, of service, of the body, of creation. All this is good, but not if it means that we neglect or underrate the Spirit. India has tended, we know, to undervalue creation and history, yet today we see Indian theologians like P. D. Devanandan and M. M. Thomas correcting the inadequate emphasis. And now surely it is the turn of the West to discover once more the meaning of the Spirit's power. The Reformation brought the Church back to the biblical teaching on grace, on faith, on justification; a whole essential part of the Christian faith was restored to its rightful place. Yet how much attention do we pay to the New Testament's repeated descriptions of the power of the Holy Spirit seen in healing, in the gift of tongues, in new life, in new men, in a transforming community? India knows much of the meaning of spirituality, yet India, like the West, has not yet tapped the full resources of the Holy Spirit, who came upon the Church at Pentecost. The transforming power of the Spirit, the joy (*ānanda*) of the *Paramātman*, can liberate and transform India, and Ireland, and the world. Not the human spirit, marvellous as that is, but the Holy Spirit, the Spirit of Jesus, coming from the triune God in Pentecostal power.

# INDEX

Abhishiktananda, Swami 15n, 69n, 78, 122n, 139
advaita 19, 25–6, 78, 82, 92, 93–5, 98, 111, 115
agape 62, 75
ahiṃsā 75, 96, 97
Allen, Roland 117
analogia entis 94
ānanda 21, 25, 57, 83, 84, 146
anāsakti 29
Anglican Church 23, 68, 119, 125
Animananda, B. 17n
Anselm 38
antaryāmin 28, 108
anubhava 76, 77–8, 82, 128
anumāna 76, 79, 138
Apologists 21, 49, 50–1, 52, 54
Apostolic Fathers 49
Appasamy, A. J. 26–9, 41, 76, 80, 90, 95, 96, 100, 105
Aquinas 24, 25, 26, 42, 64, 65, 93, 94, 122, 143
Aratoon, C. C. 33
Archibald, R. T. 27
architecture, ecclesiastical 67
Aristotle 24, 25, 42, 65
Arya Samāj 8
asat 26
āshrams 16
Athanasius 92, 99
ātman 24, 30, 74, 82
atonement 110–11
Augustine 23, 24, 56–8, 61, 91, 92, 94
Aurobindo, Sri 30, 85, 97, 107, 112
Authorised Version 61–2
avatāra 24, 25, 27, 89, 96, 107, 108, 109, 111
avyakta 50, 84

Baago, K. 12n, 17, 32, 43, 54, 69, 117n, 132, 134, 137
Baillie, D. M. 88
Baillie, John 104
Bangladesh 131
Barth, Karl 6, 24, 64–5, 90
Belfast 87, 116, 124, 131

Berkhof, Louis 67
Bernard of Clairvaux 95
Bhāgavata dharma 9
bhakti mārga 20, 26–9, 78, 80, 81, 95–6, 99, 102, 103, 107, 109, 114, 128
Boethius 56
Bonhöffer, D. 82
Boyd, R. H. 10n, 12n
Boyd, R. H. S. 18n, 30n, 121n
Brāhma Samāj 8, 20, 22, 24
Brahma Sutra 108, 109
Brahmabandhab Upadhyaya 17, 22, 24–6, 27, 32, 93, 95, 99
Brahman (the Absolute) 19, 21, 24, 25, 26, 28, 78, 83–4, 86, 91, 93–5, 97, 98, 109, 113
Brahmavidyā 86
Brethren, Church of the 44, 48
Brunner, Emil 88
Buber, Martin 56

Caesaropapism 35, 41, 69–72, 132
Calvin 41, 42, 64, 65, 68, 70, 122, 133
Carey, William 5, 7, 19, 33
caritas 62
caste 11, 12, 15, 133–4
Chaganlal Bhagwandas 33
Chakkarai, V. 96
Chalcedon 38, 88, 90
Chenchiah, P. 7, 30–2, 63, 69, 73, 107, 138, 144
Children's Special Service Mission 27
Christian Literature Society 125
Christification 112
Christology 28, 38, 50–1, 52–3, 86, 89, 98, 99, 100, 108–9, 111–13, 142
Church, Indian 10–17, 34–5, 67–9, 113, 114, 134
Church-growth 116–19, 123
Church Missionary Society 23
Church of North India 13, 35, 44–6, 124–5, 134–5
Church of South India 13, 134–5
Cicero 64
Cit 21, 25, 57, 83, 84, 98
Clarkson, William 10n

147